Sordello by Robert Browning

Robert Browning is one of the most significant Victorian Poets and, of course, English Poetry.

Much of his reputation is based upon his mastery of the dramatic monologue although his talents encompassed verse plays and even a well-regarded essay on Shelley during a long and prolific career.

He was born on May 7th, 1812 in Walmouth, London. Much of his education was home based and Browning was an eclectic and studious student, learning several languages and much else across a myriad of subjects, interests and passions.

Browning's early career began promisingly. The fragment from his intended long poem Pauline brought him to the attention of Dante Gabriel Rossetti, and was followed by Paracelsus, which was praised by both William Wordsworth and Charles Dickens. In 1840 the difficult Sordello, which was seen as willfully obscure, brought his career almost to a standstill.

Despite these artistic and professional difficulties his personal life was about to become immensely fulfilling. He began a relationship with, and then married, the older and better known Elizabeth Barrett. This new foundation served to energise his writings, his life and his career.

During their time in Italy they both wrote much of their best work. With her untimely death in 1861 he returned to London and thereafter began several further major projects.

The collection Dramatis Personae (1864) and the book-length epic poem The Ring and the Book (1868-69) were published and well received; his reputation as a venerated English poet now assured.

Robert Browning died in Venice on December 12th, 1889.

Index of Contents

PREFACE

Browning began Sordello in 1837, interrupted his work to write the earlier parts of Bells and Pomegranates, but resumed it and completed it in 1840, when it was published by Moxon. In 1863, when reprinting the poem, Browning dedicated it as below to M. Milsand, and in his dedication wrote practically a preface to the poem.

TO J. MILSAND, OF DIJON

DEAR FRIEND,—Let the next poem be introduced by your name, therefore remembered along with one of the deepest of my affections, and so repay all trouble it ever cost me. I wrote it twenty-five years ago for only a few, counting even in these on somewhat more care about its subject than they really had. My own faults of expression were many; but with care for a man or book such would be surmounted, and without it what avails the faultlessness of either? I blame nobody, least of all myself, who did my best then and since; for I lately gave time and pains to turn my work into what the many might—instead of what the few must—like; but after all, I imagined another thing at first, and therefore leave as I find it. The historical decoration was purposely of no more importance than a background requires; and my stress lay on the incidents in the development of a soul: little else is worth study. I, at least, always thought so; you, with many known and unknown to me, think so; others may one day think so; and whether my attempt remain for them or not, I trust, though away and past it, to continue ever yours,

R. B.

LONDON, June 9, 1863.

Concerning this revised edition he wrote to a friend:—

"I do not understand what—can mean by saying that Sordello has been 'rewritten.' I did certainly at one time intend to rewrite much of it, but changed my mind,—and the edition which I reprinted was the same in all respects as its predecessors—only with an elucidatory heading to each page, and some few alterations, presumably for the better, in the text, such as occur in most of my works. I cannot remember a single instance of any importance that is rewritten, and I only suppose that—has taken project for performance, and set down as 'done' what was for a while intended to be done."

For the sake of such elucidation as these head-lines give, they are introduced here as side-notes.

SORDELLO

BOOK THE FIRST

Who will, may hear Sordello's story told:
His story? Who believes me shall behold
The man, pursue his fortunes to the end,
Like me: for as the friendless-people's friend
[Sidenote: A Quixotic attempt.]
Spied from his hill-top once, despite the din
And dust of multitudes, Pentapolin
Named o' the Naked Arm, I single out
Sordello, compassed murkily about
With ravage of six long sad hundred years.
Only believe me. Ye believe?

Appears
Verona ... Never, I should warn you first,

Of my own choice had this, if not the worst
Yet not the best expedient, served to tell
A story I could body forth so well
By making speak, myself kept out of view,
The very man as he was wont to do,
And leaving you to say the rest for him.
Since, though I might be proud to see the dim
Abysmal past divide its hateful surge,
Letting of all men this one man emerge
Because it pleased me, yet, that moment past,
I should delight in watching first to last
His progress as you watch it, not a whit
More in the secret than yourselves who sit
Fresh-chapleted to listen. But it seems
Your setters-forth of unexampled themes,
Makers of quite new men, producing them,
Would best chalk broadly on each vesture's hem
The wearer's quality; or take their stand,
Motley on back and pointing-pole in hand,
Beside him. So, for once I face ye, friends,

[Sidenote: Why the Poet himself addresses his audience—]

Summoned together from the world's four ends,
Dropped down from heaven or cast up from hell,
To hear the story I propose to tell.
Confess now, poets know the dragnet's trick,
Catching the dead, if fate denies the quick,
And shaming her; 'tis not for fate to choose
Silence or song because she can refuse
Real eyes to glisten more, real hearts to ache
Less oft, real brows turn smoother for our sake:
I have experienced something of her spite;
But there 's a realm wherein she has no right
And I have many lovers. Say, but few
Friends fate accords me? Here they are: now view
The host I muster! Many a lighted face
Foul with no vestige of the grave's disgrace;
What else should tempt them back to taste our air
Except to see how their successors fare?
My audience! and they sit, each ghostly man
Striving to look as living as he can,
Brother by breathing brother; thou art set,
Clear-witted critic, by ... but I 'll not fret
A wondrous soul of them, nor move death's spleen
Who loves not to unlock them. Friends! I mean

[Sidenote: Few living, many dead.]

The living in good earnest—ye elect
Chiefly for love—suppose not I reject
Judicious praise, who contrary shall peep,
Some fit occasion, forth, for fear ye sleep,
To glean your bland approvals. Then, appear,

[Sidenote: Shelley departing, Verona appears.]

Verona! stay—thou, spirit, come not near
Now—not this time desert thy cloudy place
To scare me, thus employed, with that pure face!
I need not fear this audience, I make free
With them, but then this is no place for thee!
The thunder-phrase of the Athenian, grown
Up out of memories of Marathon,
Would echo like his own sword's griding screech
Braying a Persian shield,—the silver speech
Of Sidney's self, the starry paladin,
Turn intense as a trumpet sounding in
The knights to tilt,—wert thou to hear! What heart
Have I to play my puppets, bear my part
Before these worthies?

Lo, the past is hurled
In twain: up-thrust, out-staggering on the world,
Subsiding into shape, a darkness rears
Its outline, kindles at the core, appears
Verona. 'Tis six hundred years and more
Since an event. The Second Friedrich wore
The purple, and the Third Honorius filled
The holy chair. That autumn eve was stilled:
A last remains of sunset dimly burned
O'er the far forests, like a torch-flame turned
By the wind back upon its bearer's hand
In one long flare of crimson; as a brand,
The woods beneath lay black. A single eye
From all Verona cared for the soft sky.
But, gathering in its ancient market-place,
Talked group with restless group; and not a face
But wrath made livid, for among them were
Death's stanch purveyors, such as have in care
To feast him. Fear had long since taken root
In every breast, and now these crushed its fruit.
The ripe hate, like a wine: to note the way
It worked while each grew drunk! Men grave and gray
Stood, with shut eyelids, rocking to and fro,
[Sidenote: How her Guelfs are discomfited.]
Letting the silent luxury trickle slow
About the hollows where a heart should be;
But the young gulped with a delirious glee
Some foretaste of their first debauch in blood
At the fierce news: for, be it understood,
Envoys apprised Verona that her prince
Count Richard of Saint Boniface, joined since
A year with Azzo, Este's Lord, to thrust
Taurello Salinguerra, prime in trust
With Ecelin Romano, from his seat
Ferrara,—over-zealous in the feat
And stumbling on a peril unaware,

Was captive, trammelled in his proper snare,
They phrase it, taken by his own intrigue.
[Sidenote: Why they entreat the Lombard League,]
Immediate succor from the Lombard League
Of fifteen cities that affect the Pope,
For Azzo, therefore, and his fellow-hope
Of the Guelf cause, a glory overcast!
Men's faces, late agape, are now aghast.
"Prone is the purple pavis; Este makes
Mirth for the devil when he undertakes
To play the Ecelin; as if it cost
Merely your pushing-by to gain a post
Like his! The patron tells ye, once for all,
There be sound reasons that preferment fall
On our beloved" ...

"Duke o' the Rood, why not?"
Shouted an Estian, "grudge ye such a lot?
The hill-cat boasts some cunning of her own,
Some stealthy trick to better beasts unknown,
That quick with prey enough her hunger blunts,
And feeds her fat while gaunt the lion hunts."
"Taurello," quoth an envoy, "as in wane
Dwelt at Ferrara. Like an osprey fain
To fly but forced the earth his couch to make
Far inland, till his friend the tempest wake,
Waits he the Kaiser 's coming; and as yet
That fast friend sleeps, and he too sleeps: but let
Only the billow freshen, and he snuffs
The aroused hurricane ere it enroughs
The sea it means to cross because of him.
Sinketh the breeze? His hope-sick eye grows dim;
Creep closer on the creature! Every day
Strengthens the Pontiff; Ecelin, they say,
Dozes now at Oliero, with dry lips
Telling upon his perished finger-tips
How many ancestors are to depose
Ere he be Satan's Viceroy when the doze
Deposits him in hell. So, Guelfs rebuilt
Their houses; not a drop of blood was spilt
When Cino Bocchimpane chanced to meet
Buccio Virtù—God's wafer, and the street
Is narrow! Tutti Santi, think, a-swarm
With Ghibellins, and yet he took no harm!
This could not last. Off Salinguerra went
To Padua, Podestà, 'with pure intent,'
Said he, 'my presence, judged the single bar
To permanent tranquillity, may jar
No longer'—so! his back is fairly turned?
The pair of goodly palaces are burned,
The gardens ravaged, and our Guelfs laugh, drunk

A week with joy. The next, their laughter sunk
In sobs of blood, for they found, some strange way,
[Sidenote: In their changed fortune at Ferrara:]
Old Salinguerra back again—I say,
Old Salinguerra in the town once more
Uprooting, overturning, flame before,
Blood fetlock-high beneath him. Azzo fled;
Who 'scaped the carnage followed; then the dead
Were pushed aside from Salinguerra's throne,
He ruled once more Ferrara, all alone,
Till Azzo, stunned awhile, revived, would pounce
Coupled with Boniface, like lynx and ounce,
On the gorged bird. The burghers ground their teeth
To see troop after troop encamp beneath
I' the standing-corn thick o'er the scanty patch
It took so many patient months to snatch
Out of the marsh; while just within their walls
Men fed on men. At length Taurello calls
A parley: 'let the Count wind up the war!'
Richard, light-hearted as a plunging star,
Agrees to enter for the kindest ends
Ferrara, flanked with fifty chosen friends,
No horse-boy more, for fear your timid sort
Should fly Ferrara at the bare report.
Quietly through the town they rode, jog-jog;
'Ten, twenty, thirty,—curse the catalogue
Of burnt Guelf houses! Strange, Taurello shows
Not the least sign of life'—whereat arose
A general growl: 'How? With his victors by?
I and my Veronese? My troops and I?
Receive us, was your word?' So jogged they on,
Nor laughed their host too openly: once gone
Into the trap!"—
Six hundred years ago!
Such the time's aspect and peculiar woe
(Yourselves may spell it yet in chronicles,
Albeit the worm, our busy brother, drills
His sprawling path through letters anciently
Made fine and large to suit some abbot's eye)
When the new Hohenstauffen dropped the mask,
Flung John of Brienne's favor from his casque,
Forswore crusading, had no mind to leave
Saint Peter's proxy leisure to retrieve
Losses to Otho and to Barbaross,
Or make the Alps less easy to recross;
And, thus confirming Pope Honorius' fear,
Was excommunicate that very year.
"The triple-bearded Teuton come to life!"
Groaned the Great League; and, arming for the strife,
[Sidenote: For the times grow stormy again.]
Wide Lombardy, on tiptoe to begin,

Took up, as it was Guelf or Ghibellin,
Its cry; what cry?

"The Emperor to come!"
His crowd of feudatories, all and some,
That leapt down with a crash of swords, spears, shields,
One fighter on his fellow, to our fields,
Scattered anon, took station here and there,
And carried it, till now, with little care—
Cannot but cry for him; how else rebut
Us longer? Cliffs, an earthquake suffered jut
In the mid-sea, each domineering crest
Which naught save such another throe can wrest
From out (conceive) a certain chokeweed grown
Since o'er the waters, twine and tangle thrown
Too thick, too fast accumulating round,
Too sure to over-riot and confound
Ere long each brilliant islet with itself,
Unless a second shock save shoal and shelf,
Whirling the sea-drift wide: alas, the bruised
And sullen wreck! Sunlight to be diffused
For that! Sunlight, 'neath which, a scum at first,
The million fibres of our chokeweed nurst
Dispread themselves, mantling the troubled main,
And, shattered by those rocks, took hold again,
So kindly blazed it—that same blaze to brood
O'er every cluster of the multitude
Still hazarding new clasps, ties, filaments,
An emulous exchange of pulses, vents
Of nature into nature; till some growth
Unfancied yet, exuberantly clothe
[Sidenote: The Ghibellins' wish: the Guelfs' wish.]
A surface solid now, continuous, one:
"The Pope, for us the People, who begun
The People, carries on the People thus,
To keep that Kaiser off and dwell with us!"
See you?

Or say, Two Principles that live
Each fitly by its Representative.
"Hill-cat"—who called him so?—the gracefullest
Adventurer, the ambiguous stranger-guest
Of Lombardy (sleek but that ruffling fur,
Those talons to their sheath!) whose velvet purr
Soothes jealous neighbors when a Saxon scout
—Arpo or Yoland, is it?—one without
A country or a name, presumes to couch
Beside their noblest; until men avouch
That, of all Houses in the Trevisan,
Conrad descries no fitter, rear or van,
[Sidenote: How Ecelo's house grew head of those,]

Than Ecelo! They laughed as they enrolled
That name at Milan on the page of gold,
Godego's lord,—Ramon, Marostica,
Cartiglion, Bassano, Loria,
And every sheep-cote on the Suabian's fief!
No laughter when his son, "the Lombard Chief"
Forsooth, as Barbarossa's path was bent
To Italy along the Vale of Trent,
Welcomed him at Roncaglia! Sadness now—
The hamlets nested on the Tyrol's brow,
The Asolan and Euganean hills,
The Rhetian and the Julian, sadness fills
Them all, for Ecelin vouchsafes to stay
Among and care about them; day by day
Choosing this pinnacle, the other spot,
A castle building to defend a cot,
A cot built for a castle to defend,
Nothing but castles, castles, nor an end
To boasts how mountain ridge may join with ridge
By sunken gallery and soaring bridge.
He takes, in brief, a figure that beseems
The griesliest nightmare of the Church's dreams,
—A Signory firm-rooted, unestranged
From its old interests, and nowise changed
By its new neighborhood: perchance the vaunt
Of Otho, "my own Este shall supplant
Your Este," come to pass. The sire led in
A son as cruel; and this Ecelin
Had sons, in turn, and daughters sly and tall
And curling and compliant; but for all
Romano (so they styled him) throve, that neck
Of his so pinched and white, that hungry cheek
Proved 't was some fiend, not him, the man's-flesh went
To feed: whereas Romano's instrument,
Famous Taurello Salinguerra, sole
I' the world, a tree whose boughs were slipt the bole
Successively, why should not he shed blood
To further a design? Men understood
Living was pleasant to him as he wore
His careless surcoat, glanced some missive o'er,
Propped on his truncheon in the public way,
While his lord lifted writhen hands to pray,
Lost at Oliero's convent.

Hill-cats, face
Our Azzo, our Guelf-Lion! Why disgrace
[Sidenote: As Azzo Lord of Este heads these.]
A worthiness conspicuous near and far
(Atii at Rome while free and consular,
Este at Padua who repulsed the Hun)
By trumpeting the Church's princely son?

—Styled Patron of Rovigo's Polesine,
Ancona's march, Ferrara's ... ask, in fine,
Our chronicles, commenced when some old monk
Found it intolerable to be sunk
(Vexed to the quick by his revolting cell)
Quite out of summer while alive and well:
Ended when by his mat the Prior stood,
'Mid busy promptings of the brotherhood,
Striving to coax from his decrepit brains
The reason Father Porphyry took pains
To blot those ten lines out which used to stand
First on their charter drawn by Hildebrand.
The same night wears. Verona's rule of yore
[Sidenote: Count Richard's Palace at Verona.]
Was vested in a certain Twenty-four;
And while within his palace these debate
Concerning Richard and Ferrara's fate,
Glide we by clapping doors, with sudden glare
Of cressets vented on the dark, nor care
For aught that 's seen or heard until we shut
The smother in, the lights, all noises but
The carroch's booming: safe at last! Why strange
Such a recess should lurk behind a range
Of banquet-rooms? Your finger—thus—you push
A spring, and the wall opens, would you rush
Upon the banqueters, select your prey,
Waiting (the slaughter-weapons in the way
Strewing this very bench) with sharpened ear
A preconcerted signal to appear;
Or if you simply crouch with beating heart,
[Sidenote: Of the couple found therein,]
Bearing in some voluptuous pageant part
To startle them. Nor mutes nor masquers now;
Nor any ... does that one man sleep whose brow
The dying lamp-flame sinks and rises o'er?
What woman stood beside him? not the more
Is he unfastened from the earnest eyes
Because that arras fell between! Her wise
And lulling words are yet about the room,
Her presence wholly poured upon the gloom
Down even to her vesture's creeping stir.
And so reclines he, saturate with her,
Until an outcry from the square beneath
Pierces the charm: he springs up, glad to breathe,
Above the cunning element, and shakes
The stupor off as (look you) morning breaks
On the gay dress, and, near concealed by it,
The lean frame like a half-burnt taper, lit
Erst at some marriage-feast, then laid away
Till the Armenian bridegroom's dying day,
In his wool wedding-robe.

For he—for he,
Gate-vein of this hearts' blood of Lombardy,
(If I should falter now)—for he is thine!
Sordello, thy forerunner, Florentine!
A herald-star I know thou didst absorb
Relentless into the consummate orb
That scared it from its right to roll along
A sempiternal path with dance and song
Fulfilling its allotted period,
Serenest of the progeny of God—
Who yet resigns it not! His darling stoops
With no quenched lights, desponds with no blank troops
Of disenfranchised brilliances, for, blent
Utterly with thee, its shy element
Like thine upburneth prosperous and clear.
Still, what if I approach the august sphere
Named now with only one name, disentwine
That under-current soft and argentine
From its fierce mate in the majestic mass
Leavened as the sea whose fire was mixt with glass
In John's transcendent vision,—launch once more
That lustre? Dante, pacer of the shore
Where glutted hell disgorgeth filthiest gloom,
Unbitten by its whirring sulphur-spume—
Or whence the grieved and obscure waters slope
Into a darkness quieted by hope;
Plucker of amaranths grown beneath God's eye
In gracious twilights where his chosen lie,—
I would do this! If I should falter now!
[Sidenote: One belongs to Dante; his Birthplace.]
In Mantua territory half is slough,
Half pine-tree forest; maples, scarlet oaks
Breed o'er the river-beds; even Mincio chokes
With sand the summer through: but 't is morass
In winter up to Mantua walls. There was,
Some thirty years before this evening's coil,
One spot reclaimed from the surrounding spoil,
Goito; just a castle built amid
A few low mountains; firs and larches hid
Their main defiles, and rings of vineyard bound
The rest. Some captured creature in a pound,
Whose artless wonder quite precludes distress,
Secure beside in its own loveliness,
So peered with airy head, below, above,
The castle at its toils, the lapwings love
To glean among at grape-time. Pass within.
A maze of corridors contrived for sin,
Dusk winding-stairs, dim galleries got past,
You gain the inmost chambers, gain at last
A maple-panelled room: that haze which seems

Floating about the panel, if there gleams
A sunbeam over it, will turn to gold
And in light-graven characters unfold
The Arab's wisdom everywhere; what shade
Marred them a moment, those slim pillars made,
Cut like a company of palms to prop
The roof, each kissing top entwined with top,
Leaning together; in the carver's mind
Some knot of bacchanals, flushed cheek combined
With straining forehead, shoulders purpled, hair
Diffused between, who in a goat-skin bear
A vintage; graceful sister-palms! But quick
To the main wonder, now. A vault, see; thick
[Sidenote: A Vault inside the Castle at Goito,]
Black shade about the ceiling, though fine slits
Across the buttress suffer light by fits
Upon a marvel in the midst. Nay, stoop—
A dullish gray-streaked cumbrous font, a group
Round it,—each side of it, where'er one sees,—
Upholds it; shrinking Caryatides
Of just-tinged marble like Eve's lilied flesh
Beneath her maker's finger when the fresh
First pulse of life shot brightening the snow.
The font's edge burdens every shoulder, so
They muse upon the ground, eyelids half closed;
Some, with meek arms behind their backs disposed,
Some, crossed above their bosoms, some, to veil
Their eyes, some, propping chin and cheek so pale,
Some, hanging slack an utter helpless length
Dead as a buried vestal whose whole strength
Goes when the grate above shuts heavily.
So dwell these noiseless girls, patient to see,
Like priestesses because of sin impure
Penanced forever, who resigned endure,
Having that once drunk sweetness to the dregs.
And every eve, Sordello's visit begs
Pardon for them: constant as eve he came
To sit beside each in her turn, the same
As one of them, a certain space: and awe
[Sidenote: And what Sordello would see there.]
Made a great indistinctness till he saw
Sunset slant cheerful through the buttress-chinks,
Gold seven times globed; surely our maiden shrinks
And a smile stirs her as if one faint grain
Her load were lightened, one shade less the stain
Obscured her forehead, yet one more bead slipt
From off the rosary whereby the crypt
Keeps count of the contritions of its charge?
Then with a step more light, a heart more large,
He may depart, leave her and every one
To linger out the penance in mute stone.

Ah, but Sordello? 'T is the tale I mean
To tell you.

In this castle may be seen,
On the hill-tops, or underneath the vines,
Or eastward by the mound of firs and pines
That shuts out Mantua, still in loneliness,
A slender boy in a loose page's dress,
Sordello: do but look on him awhile
Watching ('t is autumn) with an earnest smile
The noisy flock of thievish birds at work
Among the yellowing vineyards; see him lurk
[Sidenote: His boyhood in the domain of Ecelin.]
('T is winter with its sullenest of storms)
Beside that arras-length of broidered forms,
On tiptoe, lifting in both hands a light
Which makes yon warrior's visage flutter bright
—Ecelo, dismal father of the brood,
And Ecelin, close to the girl he wooed,
Auria, and their Child, with all his wives
From Agnes to the Tuscan that survives,
Lady of the castle, Adelaide. His face
—Look, now he turns away! Yourselves shall trace
(The delicate nostril swerving wide and fine,
A sharp and restless lip, so well combine
With that calm brow) a soul fit to receive
Delight at every sense; you can believe
Sordello foremost in the regal class
Nature has broadly severed from her mass
Of men, and framed for pleasure, as she frames
Some happy lands, that have luxurious names,
For loose fertility; a footfall there
Suffices to upturn to the warm air
Half-germinating spices; mere decay
Produces richer life; and day by day
New pollen on the lily-petal grows,
And still more labyrinthine buds the rose.
You recognize at once the finer dress
Of flesh that amply lets in loveliness
At eye and ear, while round the rest is furled
(As though she would not trust them with her world)
A veil that shows a sky not near so blue,
And lets but half the sun look fervid through.
[Sidenote: How a poet's soul comes into play.]
How can such love?—like souls on each full-fraught
Discovery brooding, blind at first to aught
Beyond its beauty, till exceeding love
Becomes an aching weight; and, to remove
A curse that haunts such natures—to preclude
Their finding out themselves can work no good
To what they love nor make it very blest

By their endeavor,—they are fain invest
The lifeless thing with life from their own soul,
Availing it to purpose, to control,
To dwell distinct and have peculiar joy
And separate interests that may employ
That beauty fitly, for its proper sake.
Nor rest they here; fresh births of beauty wake
Fresh homage, every grade of love is past,
With every mode of loveliness: then cast
Inferior idols off their borrowed crown
Before a coming glory. Up and down
Runs arrowy fire, while earthly forms combine
To throb the secret forth; a touch divine—
And the sealed eyeball owns the mystic rod;
Visibly through his garden walketh God.
[Sidenote: What denotes such a soul's progress.]
So fare they. Now revert. One character
Denotes them through the progress and the stir,—
A need to blend with each external charm,
Bury themselves, the whole heart wide and warm,—
In something not themselves; they would belong
To what they worship—stronger and more strong
Thus prodigally fed—which gathers shape
And feature, soon imprisons past escape
The votary framed to love and to submit
Nor ask, as passionate he kneels to it,
Whence grew the idol's empery. So runs
A legend; light had birth ere moons and suns,
Flowing through space a river and alone,
Till chaos burst and blank the spheres were strown
Hither and thither, foundering and blind:
When into each of them rushed light—to find
Itself no place, foiled of its radiant chance.
Let such forego their just inheritance!
For there 's a class that eagerly looks, too,
On beauty, but, unlike the gentler crew,
Proclaims each new revealment born a twin
With a distinctest consciousness within,
Referring still the quality, now first
Revealed, to their own soul—its instinct nursed
In silence, now remembered better, shown
More thoroughly, but not the less their own;
A dream come true; the special exercise
[Sidenote: How poets class at length—]
Of any special function that implies
The being fair, or good, or wise, or strong,
Dormant within their nature all along—
Whose fault? So, homage, other souls direct
Without, turns inward. "How should this deject
Thee, soul?" they murmur; "wherefore strength be quelled
Because, its trivial accidents withheld,

Organs are missed that clog the world, inert,
Wanting a will, to quicken and exert,
Like thine—existence cannot satiate,
Cannot surprise? Laugh thou at envious fate,
Who, from earth's simplest combination stampt
With individuality—uncrampt
By living its faint elemental life,
Dost soar to heaven's complexest essence, rife
With grandeurs, unaffronted to the last,
[Sidenote: For honor,]
Equal to being all!"

In truth? Thou hast
Life, then—wilt challenge life for us: our race
Is vindicated so, obtains its place
In thy ascent, the first of us; whom we
[Sidenote: Or shame—]
May follow, to the meanest, finally,
With our more bounded wills?

Ah, but to find
A certain mood enervate such a mind,
Counsel it slumber in the solitude
Thus reached, nor, stooping, task for mankind's good
Its nature just as life and time accord
"—Too narrow an arena to reward
Emprise—the world's occasion worthless since
Not absolutely fitted to evince
Its mastery!" Or if yet worse befall,
And a desire possess it to put all
That nature forth, forcing our straitened sphere
Contain it,—to display completely here
The mastery another life should learn,
Thrusting in time eternity's concern,—
So that Sordello ...
[Sidenote: Which may the Gods avert]

Fool, who spied the mark
Of leprosy upon him, violet-dark
Already as he loiters? Born just now,
With the new century, beside the glow
And efflorescence out of barbarism;
Witness a Greek or two from the abysm
That stray through Florence-town with studious air,
Calming the chisel of that Pisan pair:
If Nicolo should carve a Christus yet!
While at Siena is Guidone set,
Forehead on hand; a painful birth must be
Matured ere Saint Eufemia's sacristy
Or transept gather fruits of one great gaze
At the moon: look you! The same orange haze,—

The same blue stripe round that—and, in the midst,
Thy spectral whiteness, Mother-maid, who didst
Pursue the dizzy painter!

Woe, then, worth
Any officious babble letting forth
The leprosy confirmed and ruinous
To spirit lodged in a contracted house!
Go back to the beginning, rather; blend
It gently with Sordello's life; the end
Is piteous, you may see, but much between
Pleasant enough. Meantime, some pyx to screen
The full-grown pest, some lid to shut upon
The goblin! So they found at Babylon,
(Colleagues, mad Lucius and sage Antonine)
Sacking the city, by Apollo's shrine,
In rummaging among the rarities,
A certain coffer; he who made the prize
Opened it greedily; and out there curled
Just such another plague, for half the world
Was stung. Crawl in then, hag, and couch asquat,
Keeping that blotchy bosom thick in spot
Until your time is ripe! The coffer-lid
Is fastened, and the coffer safely hid
Under the Loxian's choicest gifts of gold.
Who will may hear Sordello's story told,
And now he never could remember when
He dwelt not at Goito. Calmly, then,
[Sidenote: From Sordello, now in childhood.]
About this secret lodge of Adelaide's
Glided his youth away; beyond the glades
On the fir-forest border, and the rim
Of the low range of mountain, was for him
No other world: but this appeared his own
To wander through at pleasure and alone.
The castle too seemed empty; far and wide
Might he disport; only the northern side
Lay under a mysterious interdict—
Slight, just enough remembered to restrict
His roaming to the corridors, the vault
Where those font-bearers expiate their fault,
The maple-chamber, and the little nooks
And nests, and breezy parapet that looks
Over the woods to Mantua: there he strolled.
Some foreign women-servants, very old,
Tended and crept about him—all his clue
To the world's business and embroiled ado
Distant a dozen hill-tops at the most.
[Sidenote: The delights of his childish fancy,]
And first a simple sense of life engrossed
Sordello in his drowsy Paradise;

The day's adventures for the day suffice—
Its constant tribute of perceptions strange.
With sleep and stir in healthy interchange,
Suffice, and leave him for the next at ease
Like the great palmer-worm that strips the trees,
Eats the life out of every luscious plant,
And, when September finds them sere or scant,
Puts forth two wondrous winglets, alters quite,
And hies him after unforeseen delight.
So fed Sordello, not a shard dissheathed;
As ever, round each new discovery, wreathed
Luxuriantly the fancies infantine
His admiration, bent on making fine
Its novel friend at any risk, would fling
In gay profusion forth; a ficklest king,
Confessed those minions!—eager to dispense
So much from his own stock of thought and sense
As might enable each to stand alone
And serve him for a fellow; with his own,
Joining the qualities that just before
Had graced some older favorite. Thus they wore
A fluctuating halo, yesterday
Set flicker and to-morrow filched away,—
Those upland objects each of separate name,
Each with an aspect never twice the same,
Waxing and waning as the new-born host
Of fancies, like a single night's hoar-frost,
[Sidenote: Which could blow out a great bubble,]
Gave to familiar things a face grotesque;
Only, preserving through the mad burlesque
A grave regard. Conceive! the orpine patch
Blossoming earliest on the log-house thatch
The day those archers wound along the vines—
Related to the Chief that left their lines
To climb with clinking step the northern stair
Up to the solitary chambers where
Sordello never came. Thus thrall reached thrall;
He o'er-festooning every interval,
As the adventurous spider, making light
Of distance, shoots her threads from depth to height,
From barbican to battlement: so flung
Fantasies forth and in their centre swung
Our architect,—the breezy morning fresh
Above, and merry,—all his waving mesh
Laughing with lucid dew-drops rainbow-edged.
This world of ours by tacit pact is pledged
To laying such a spangled fabric low
Whether by gradual brush or gallant blow.
But its abundant will was balked here: doubt
[Sidenote: Being secure awhile from intrusion.]
Rose tardily in one so fenced about

From most that nurtures judgment, care and pain:
Judgment, that dull expedient we are fain,
Less favored, to adopt betimes and force
Stead us, diverted from our natural course
Of joys—contrive some yet amid the dearth,
Vary and render them, it may be, worth
Most we forego. Suppose Sordello hence
Selfish enough, without a moral sense
However feeble; what informed the boy
Others desired a portion in his joy?
Or say a ruthful chance broke woof and warp—
A heron's nest beat down by March winds sharp,
A fawn breathless beneath the precipice,
A bird with unsoiled breast and unfilmed eyes
Warm in the brake—could these undo the trance
Lapping Sordello? Not a circumstance
That makes for you, friend Naddo! Eat fern-seed
And peer beside us and report indeed
If (your word) "genius" dawned with throes and stings
And the whole fiery catalogue, while springs,
Summers and winters quietly came and went.
Time put at length that period to content,
By right the world should have imposed: bereft
Of its good offices, Sordello, left
To study his companions, managed rip
Their fringe off, learn the true relationship,
Core with its crust, their nature with his own:
Amid his wild-wood sights he lived alone.
As if the poppy felt with him! Though he
Partook the poppy's red effrontery
Till Autumn spoiled their fleering quite with rain,
And, turbanless, a coarse brown rattling crane
Lay bare. That 's gone: yet why renounce, for that,
His disenchanted tributaries—flat
Perhaps, but scarce so utterly forlorn,
Their simple presence might not well be borne
Whose parley was a transport once: recall
The poppy's gifts, it flaunts you, after all,
A poppy:—why distrust the evidence
Of each soon satisfied and healthy sense?
[Sidenote: But it comes; and new-born judgment]
The new-born judgment answered, "little boots
Beholding other creatures' attributes
And having none!" or, say that it sufficed,
"Yet, could one but possess, one's self," (enticed
Judgment) "some special office!" Naught beside
Serves you? "Well then, be somehow justified
For this ignoble wish to circumscribe
And concentrate, rather than swell, the tribe
Of actual pleasures: what, now, from without
Effects it?—proves, despite a lurking doubt,

Mere sympathy sufficient, trouble spared?
That, tasting joys by proxy thus, you fared
[Sidenote: Decides that he needs sympathizers.]
The better for them?" Thus much craved his soul.
Alas, from the beginning love is whole
And true; if sure of naught beside, most sure
Of its own truth at least; nor may endure
A crowd to see its face, that cannot know
How hot the pulses throb its heart below.
While its own helplessness and utter want
Of means to worthily be ministrant
To what it worships, do but fan the more
Its flame, exalt the idol far before
Itself as it would have it ever be.
Souls like Sordello, on the contrary,
Coerced and put to shame, retaining will,
Care little, take mysterious comfort still,
But look forth tremblingly to ascertain
If others judge their claims not urged in vain,
And say for them their stifled thoughts aloud.
So, they must ever live before a crowd:
—"Vanity," Naddo tells you.

Whence contrive
A crowd, now? From these women just alive,
That archer-troop? Forth glided—not alone
Each painted warrior, every girl of stone,
Nor Adelaide (bent double o'er a scroll,
One maiden at her knees, that eve, his soul
Shook as he stumbled through the arras'd glooms
On them, for, 'mid quaint robes and weird perfumes,
Started the meagre Tuscan up,—her eyes,
The maiden's, also, bluer with surprise)
—But the entire out-world: whatever, scraps
And snatches, song and story, dreams perhaps,
Conceited the world's offices, and he
Had hitherto transferred to flower or tree,
Not counted a befitting heritage
Each, of its own right, singly to engage
Some man, no other,—such now dared to stand
Alone. Strength, wisdom, grace on every hand
Soon disengaged themselves, and he discerned
A sort of human life: at least, was turned
[Sidenote: He therefore creates such a company;]
A stream of lifelike figures through his brain.
Lord, liegeman, valvassor and suzerain,
Ere he could choose, surrounded him; a stuff
To work his pleasure on; there, sure enough:
But as for gazing, what shall fix that gaze?
Are they to simply testify the ways
He who convoked them sends his soul along

With the cloud's thunder or a dove's brood-song?
—While they live each his life, boast each his own
[Sidenote: Each of which, leading its own life,]
Peculiar dower of bliss, stand each alone
In some one point where something dearest loved
Is easiest gained—far worthier to be proved
Than aught he envies in the forest-wights!
No simple and self-evident delights,
But mixed desires of unimagined range,
Contrasts or combinations, new and strange,
Irksome perhaps, yet plainly recognized
By this, the sudden company—loves prized
By those who are to prize his own amount
Of loves. Once care because such make account,
Allow that foreign recognitions stamp
The current value, and his crowd shall vamp
Him counterfeits enough; and so their print
Be on the piece, 'tis gold, attests the mint.
And "good," pronounce they whom his new appeal
Is made to: if their casual print conceal—
This arbitrary good of theirs o'ergloss
What he has lived without, nor felt the loss—
Qualities strange, ungainly, wearisome,
—What matter? So must speech expand the dumb
Part-sigh, part-smile with which Sordello, late
Whom no poor woodland-sights could satiate,
Betakes himself to study hungrily
Just what the puppets his crude fantasy
Supposes notablest,—popes, kings, priests, knights,—
May please to promulgate for appetites;
Accepting all their artificial joys
Not as he views them, but as he employs
Each shape to estimate the other's stock
Of attributes, whereon—a marshalled flock
Of authorized enjoyments—he may spend
Himself, be men, now, as he used to blend
With tree and flower—nay more entirely, else
'T were mockery: for instance, "How excels
My life that chieftain's?" (who apprised the youth
Ecelin, here, becomes this month, in truth,
Imperial Vicar?) "Turns he in his tent
Remissly? Be it so—my head is bent
Deliciously amid my girls to sleep.
What if he stalks the Trentine-pass? Yon steep
I climbed an hour ago with little toil:
We are alike there. But can I, too, foil
The Guelf's paid stabber, carelessly afford
Saint Mark's a spectacle, the sleight o' the sword
Baffling the treason in a moment?" Here
No rescue! Poppy he is none, but peer
To Ecelin, assuredly: his hand,

Fashioned no otherwise, should wield a brand
With Ecelin's success—try, now! He soon
Was satisfied, returned as to the moon
From earth: left each abortive boy's attempt
[Sidenote: Has qualities impossible to a boy,]
For feats, from failure happily exempt,
In fancy at his beck. "One day I will
Accomplish it! Are they not older still
—Not grown up men and women? 'T is beside
Only a dream; and though I must abide
With dreams now, I may find a thorough vent
For all myself, acquire an instrument
For acting what these people act; my soul
Hunting a body out may gain its whole
Desire some day!" How else express chagrin
And resignation, show the hope steal in
With which he let sink from an aching wrist
The rough-hewn ash-bow? Straight, a gold shaft hissed
Into the Syrian air, struck Malek down
Superbly! "Crosses to the breach! God's Town
Is gained him back!" Why bend rough ash-bows more?
Thus lives he: if not careless as before,
Comforted: for one may anticipate,
Rehearse the future, be prepared when fate
Shall have prepared in turn real men whose names
Startle, real places of enormous fames,
Este abroad and Ecelin at home
To worship him,—Mantua, Verona, Rome
To witness it. Who grudges time so spent?
Rather test qualities to heart's content—
Summon them, thrice selected, near and far—
Compress the starriest into one star,
[Sidenote: So, only to be appropriated in fancy,]
And grasp the whole at once!

The pageant thinned
Accordingly; from rank to rank, like wind
His spirit passed to winnow and divide;
Back fell the simpler phantasms; every side
The strong clave to the wise; with either classed
The beauteous; so, till two or three amassed
Mankind's beseemingnesses, and reduced
Themselves eventually, graces loosed,
Strengths lavished, all to heighten up One Shape
Whose potency no creature should escape.
Can it be Friedrich of the bowmen's talk?
Surely that grape-juice, bubbling at the stalk,
Is some gray scorching Sarasenic wine
The Kaiser quaffs with the Miramoline—
Those swarthy hazel-clusters, seamed and chapped,
Or filberts russet-sheathed and velvet-capped,

Are dates plucked from the bough John Brienne sent,
To keep in mind his sluggish armament
Of Canaan:—Friedrich's, all the pomp and fierce
Demeanor! But harsh sounds and sights transpierce
So rarely the serene cloud where he dwells,
[Sidenote: And practised on till the real come.]
Whose looks enjoin, whose lightest words are spells
On the obdurate! That right arm indeed
Has thunder for its slave; but where 's the need
Of thunder if the stricken multitude
Hearkens, arrested in its angriest mood,
While songs go up exulting, then dispread,
Dispart, disperse, lingering overhead
Like an escape of angels? 'T is the tune,
Nor much unlike the words his women croon
Smilingly, colorless and faint-designed
Each, as a worn-out queen's face some remind
Of her extreme youth's love-tales. "Eglamor
Made that!" Half minstrel and half emperor,
What but ill objects vexed him? Such he slew.
The kinder sort were easy to subdue
By those ambrosial glances, dulcet tones;
And these a gracious hand advanced to thrones
Beneath him. Wherefore twist and torture this,
Striving to name afresh the antique bliss,
Instead of saying, neither less nor more,
[Sidenote: He means to be perfect—say, Apollo;]
He had discovered, as our world before,
Apollo? That shall be the name; nor bid
Me rag by rag expose how patchwork hid
The youth—what thefts of every clime and day
Contributed to purfle the array
He climbed with (June at deep) some close ravine
'Mid clatter of its million pebbles sheen,
Over which, singing soft, the runnel slipped
Elate with rains: into whose streamlet dipped
He foot, yet trod, you thought, with unwet sock—
Though really on the stubs of living rock
Ages ago it crenelled; vines for roof,
Lindens for wall; before him, aye aloof,
Flittered in the cool some azure damsel-fly,
Born of the simmering quiet, there to die.
Emerging whence, Apollo still, he spied
Mighty descents of forest; multiplied
Tuft on tuft, here, the frolic myrtle-trees,
There gendered the grave maple stocks at ease,
And, proud of its observer, straight the wood
Tried old surprises on him; black it stood
A sudden barrier ('t was a cloud passed o'er)
So dead and dense, the tiniest brute no more
Must pass; yet presently (the cloud dispatched)

Each clump, behold, was glistening detached
A shrub, oak-boles shrunk into ilex-stems!
Yet could not he denounce the stratagems
He saw thro', till, hours thence, aloft would hang
White summer-lightnings; as it sank and sprang
To measure, that whole palpitating breast
Of heaven, 't was Apollo, nature prest
At eve to worship.

Time stole: by degrees
The Pythons perish off; his votaries
Sink to respectful distance; songs redeem
Their pains, but briefer; their dismissals seem
Emphatic; only girls are very slow
To disappear—his Delians! Some that glow
O' the instant, more with earlier loves to wrench
Away, reserves to quell, disdains to quench;
Alike in one material circumstance—
All soon or late adore Apollo! Glance
The bevy through, divine Apollo's choice,
[Sidenote: And Apollo must one day find Daphne.]
His Daphne! "We secure Count Richard's voice
In Este's counsels, good for Este's ends
As our Taurello," say his faded friends,
"By granting him our Palma!"—the sole child,
They mean, of Agnes Este who beguiled
Ecelin, years before this Adelaide
Wedded and turned him wicked: "but the maid
Rejects his suit," those sleepy women boast.
She, scorning all beside, deserves the most
Sordello: so, conspicuous in his world
Of dreams sat Palma. How the tresses curled
Into a sumptuous swell of gold and wound
About her like a glory! even the ground
Was bright as with spilt sunbeams; breathe not, breathe
Not!—poised, see, one leg doubled underneath,
Its small foot buried in the dimpling snow,
Rests, but the other, listlessly below,
O'er the couch-side swings feeling for cool air,
The vein-streaks swollen a richer violet where
The languid blood lies heavily; yet calm
On her slight prop, each flat and outspread palm,
As but suspended in the act to rise
By consciousness of beauty, whence her eyes
[Sidenote: But when will this dream turn truth?]
Turn with so frank a triumph, for she meets
Apollo's gaze in the pine glooms.

Time fleets:
That 's worst! Because the pre-appointed age
Approaches. Fate is tardy with the stage

And crowd she promised. Lean he grows and pale,
Though restlessly at rest. Hardly avail
Fancies to soothe him. Time steals, yet alone
He tarries here! The earnest smile is gone.
How long this might continue matters not;
[Sidenote: For the time is ripe, and he ready.]
—Forever, possibly; since to the spot
None come: our lingering Taurello quits
Mantua at last, and light our lady flits
Back to her place disburdened of a care.
Strange—to be constant here if he is there!
Is it distrust? Oh, never! for they both
Goad Ecelin alike, Romano's growth
Is daily manifest, with Azzo dumb
And Richard wavering: let but Friedrich come,
Find matter for the minstrelsy's report!
—Lured from the Isle and its young Kaiser's court
To sing us a Messina morning up,
And, double rillet of a drinking cup,
Sparkle along to ease the land of drouth,
Northward to Provence that, and thus far south
The other. What a method to apprise
Neighbors of births, espousals, obsequies!
Which in their very tongue the Troubadour
Records; and his performance makes a tour,
For Trouveres bear the miracle about,
Explain its cunning to the vulgar rout,
Until the Formidable House is famed
Over the country—as Taurello aimed,
Who introduced, although the rest adopt,
The novelty. Such games, her absence stopped,
Begin afresh now Adelaide, recluse
No longer, in the light of day pursues
Her plans at Mantua: whence an accident
Which, breaking on Sordello's mixed content,
Opened, like any flash that cures the blind,
The veritable business of mankind.

BOOK THE SECOND

The woods were long austere with snow: at last
[Sidenote: This bubble of fancy.]
Pink leaflets budded on the beech, and fast
Larches, scattered through pine-tree solitudes,
Brightened, "as in the slumbrous heart o' the woods
Our buried year, a witch, grew young again
To placid incantations, and that stain
About were from her caldron, green smoke blent
With those black pines"—so Eglamor gave vent

To a chance fancy. Whence a just rebuke
From his companion; brother Naddo shook
The solemnest of brows; "Beware," he said,
"Of setting up conceits in nature's stead!"
Forth wandered our Sordello. Naught so sure
As that to-day's adventure will secure
Palma, the visioned lady—only pass
O'er yon damp mound and its exhausted grass,
Under that brake where sundawn feeds the stalks
Of withered fern with gold, into those walks
Of pine and take her! Buoyantly he went.
Again his stooping forehead was besprent
With dew-drops from the skirting ferns. Then wide
Opened the great morass, shot every side
With flashing water through and through; a-shine,
Thick steaming, all alive. Whose shape divine,
Quivered i' the farthest rainbow-vapor, glanced
Athwart the flying herons? He advanced,
But warily; though Mincio leaped no more,
Each footfall burst up in the marish-floor
A diamond jet: and if he stopped to pick
Rose-lichen, or molest the leeches quick,
And circling blood-worms, minnow, newt or loach,
A sudden pond would silently encroach
This way and that. On Palma passed. The verge
Of a new wood was gained. She will emerge
Flushed, now, and panting,—crowds to see,—will own
She loves him—Boniface to hear, to groan,
To leave his suit! One screen of pine-trees still
Opposes: but—the startling spectacle—
Mantua, this time! Under the walls—a crowd
Indeed, real men and women, gay and loud
Round a pavilion. How he stood!

In truth
[Sidenote: When greatest and brightest, bursts.]
No prophecy had come to pass: his youth
In its prime now—and where was homage poured
Upon Sordello?—born to be adored,
And suddenly discovered weak, scarce made
To cope with any, cast into the shade
By this and this. Yet something seemed to prick
And tingle in his blood; a sleight—a trick—
And much would be explained. It went for naught—
The best of their endowments were ill bought
With his identity: nay, the conceit,
That this day's roving led to Palma's feet
Was not so vain—list! The word, "Palma!" Steal
Aside, and die, Sordello; this is real,
And this—abjure!

What next? The curtains see
Dividing! She is there; and presently
He will be there—the proper You, at length—
In your own cherished dress of grace and strength:
Most like, the very Boniface!

Not so.
It was a showy man advanced; but though
A glad cry welcomed him, then every sound
Sank and the crowd disposed themselves around,
—"This is not he," Sordello felt; while, "Place
For the best Troubadour of Boniface!"
Hollaed the Jongleurs,—"Eglamor, whose lay
Concludes his patron's Court of Love to-day!"
Obsequious Naddo strung the master's lute
With the new lute-string, "Elys," named to suit
[Sidenote: At a Court of Love a minstrel sings.]
The song: he stealthily at watch, the while,
Biting his lip to keep down a great smile
Of pride: then up he struck. Sordello's brain
Swam; for he knew a sometime deed again;
So, could supply each foolish gap and chasm
The minstrel left in his enthusiasm,
Mistaking its true version—was the tale
Not of Apollo? Only, what avail
Luring her down, that Elys an he pleased,
If the man dared no further? Has he ceased?
And, lo, the people's frank applause half done,
Sordello was beside him, had begun
(Spite of indignant twitchings from his friend
The Trouvere) the true lay with the true end,
Taking the other's names and time and place
For his. On flew the song, a giddy race,
[Sidenote: Sordello, before Palma, conquers him,]
After the flying story; word made leap
Out word, rhyme—rhyme; the lay could barely keep
Pace with the action visibly rushing past:
Both ended. Back fell Naddo more aghast
Than some Egyptian from the harassed bull
That wheeled abrupt and, bellowing, fronted full
His plague, who spied a scarab 'neath the tongue,
And found 't was Apis' flank his hasty prong
Insulted. But the people—but the cries,
The crowding round, and proffering the prize!
—For he had gained some prize. He seemed to shrink
Into a sleepy cloud, just at whose brink
One sight withheld him. There sat Adelaide,
Silent; but at her knees the very maid
Of the North Chamber, her red lips as rich,
The same pure fleecy hair; one weft of which,
Golden and great, quite touched his cheek as o'er

She leant, speaking some six words and no more.
He answered something, anything; and she
Unbound a scarf and laid it heavily
Upon him, her neck's warmth and all. Again
Moved the arrested magic; in his brain
Noises grew, and a light that turned to glare,
And greater glare, until the intense flare
Engulfed him, shut the whole scene from his sense.
And when he woke 't was many a furlong thence,
At home; the sun shining his ruddy wont;
The customary birds'-chirp; but his front
[Sidenote: Receives the prize, and ruminates.]
Was crowned—was crowned! Her scented scarf around
His neck! Whose gorgeous vesture heaps the ground?
A prize? He turned, and peeringly on him
Brooded the women-faces, kind and dim,
Ready to talk—"The Jongleurs in a troop
Had brought him back, Naddo and Squarcialupe
And Tagliafer; how strange! a childhood spent
In taking, well for him, so brave a bent!
Since Eglamor," they heard, "was dead with spite,
And Palma chose him for her minstrel."

Light
Sordello rose—to think, now; hitherto
He had perceived. Sure, a discovery grew
Out of it all! Best live from first to last
The transport o'er again. A week he passed,
Sucking the sweet out of each circumstance,
From the bard's outbreak to the luscious trance
Bounding his own achievement. Strange! A man
Recounted an adventure, but began
Imperfectly; his own task was to fill
The framework up, sing well what he sung ill,
Supply the necessary points, set loose
As many incidents of little use
—More imbecile the other, not to see
Their relative importance clear as he!
But, for a special pleasure in the act
Of singing—had he ever turned, in fact,
From Elys, to sing Elys?—from each fit
Of rapture to contrive a song of it?
True, this snatch or the other seemed to wind
Into a treasure, helped himself to find
A beauty in himself; for, see, he soared
By means of that mere snatch, to many a hoard
Of fancies; as some falling cone hears soft
The eye along the fir-tree spire, aloft
To a dove's nest. Then, how divine the cause
Why such performance should exact applause
From men, if they had fancies too? Did fate

Decree they found a beauty separate
In the poor snatch itself?—"Take Elys, there,
—'Her head that's sharp and perfect like a pear,
So close and smooth are laid the few fine locks
Colored like honey oozed from topmost rocks
Sun-blanched the livelong summer'—if they heard
Just those two rhymes, assented at my word,
And loved them as I love them who have run
These fingers through those pale locks, let the sun
Into the white cool skin—who first could clutch,
Then praise—I needs must be a god to such.
Or what if some, above themselves, and yet
[Sidenote: How had he been superior to Eglamor?]
Beneath me, like their Eglamor, have set
An impress on our gift? So, men believe
And worship what they know not, nor receive
Delight from. Have they fancies—slow, perchance,
Not at their beck, which indistinctly glance
Until, by song, each floating part be linked
To each, and all grow palpable, distinct?"
He pondered this.

Meanwhile, sounds low and drear
Stole on him, and a noise of footsteps, near
And nearer, while the underwood was pushed
Aside, the larches grazed, the dead leaves crushed
At the approach of men. The wind seemed laid;
Only, the trees shrunk slightly and a shade
Came o'er the sky although 't was mid-day yet:
You saw each half-shut downcast floweret
Flutter—"a Roman bride, when they 'd dispart
Her unbound tresses with the Sabine dart,
Holding that famous rape in memory still,
Felt creep into her curls the iron chill,
And looked thus," Eglamor would say—indeed
[Sidenote: This is answered by Eglamor himself:]
'T is Eglamor, no other, these precede
Home hither in the woods. "'T were surely sweet
Far from the scene of one's forlorn defeat
To sleep!" judged Naddo, who in person led
Jongleurs and Trouveres, chanting at their head,
A scanty company; for, sooth to say,
Our beaten Troubadour had seen his day.
Old worshippers were something shamed, old friends
Nigh weary; still the death proposed amends.
"Let us but get them safely through my song
And home again!" quoth Naddo.

All along,
This man (they rest the bier upon the sand)
—This calm corpse with the loose flowers in his hand,

Eglamor, lived Sordello's opposite.
For him indeed was Naddo's notion right,
And verse a temple-worship vague and vast,
A ceremony that withdrew the last
Opposing bolt, looped back the lingering veil
Which hid the holy place: should one so frail
Stand there without such effort? or repine
If much was blank, uncertain at the shrine
He knelt before, till, soothed by many a rite,
The power responded, and some sound or sight
Grew up, his own forever, to be fixed,
In rhyme, the beautiful, forever!—mixed
With his own life, unloosed when he should please,
[Sidenote: One who belonged to what he loved,]
Having it safe at hand, ready to ease
All pain, remove all trouble; every time
He loosed that fancy from its bonds of rhyme,
(Like Perseus when he loosed his naked love)
Faltering; so distinct and far above
Himself, these fancies! He, no genius rare,
Transfiguring in fire or wave or air
At will, but a poor gnome that, cloistered up
In some rock-chamber with his agate cup,
His topaz rod, his seed-pearl, in these few
And their arrangement finds enough to do
For his best art. Then, how he loved that art!
The calling marking him a man apart
From men—one not to care, take counsel for
Cold hearts, comfortless faces—(Eglamor
Was neediest of his tribe)—since verse, the gift,
Was his, and men, the whole of them, must shift
Without it, e'en content themselves with wealth
And pomp and power, snatching a life by stealth.
So, Eglamor was not without his pride!
[Sidenote: Loving his art and rewarded by it,]
The sorriest bat which cowers throughout noontide
While other birds are jocund, has one time
When moon and stars are blinded, and the prime
Of earth is his to claim, nor find a peer;
And Eglamor was noblest poet here—
He well knew, 'mid those April woods, he cast
Conceits upon in plenty as he passed,
That Naddo might suppose him not to think
Entirely on the coming triumph: wink
At the one weakness! 'Twas a fervid child,
That song of his; no brother of the guild
Had e'er conceived its like. The rest you know,
The exaltation and the overthrow:
Our poet lost his purpose, lost his rank,
His life—to that it came. Yet envy sank
Within him, as he heard Sordello out,

And, for the first time, shouted—tried to shout
Like others, not from any zeal to show
Pleasure that way: the common sort did so.
What else was Eglamor? who, bending down
As they, placed his beneath Sordello's crown,
Printed a kiss on his successor's hand,
Left one great tear on it, then joined his band
—In time; for some were watching at the door:
Who knows what envy may effect? "Give o'er,
Nor charm his lips, nor craze him!" (here one spied
And disengaged the withered crown)—"Beside
His crown? How prompt and clear those verses rang
To answer yours! nay, sing them!" And he sang
Them calmly. Home he went; friends used to wait
His coming, zealous to congratulate;
But, to a man,—so quickly runs report,—
Could do no less than leave him, and escort
His rival. That eve, then, bred many a thought:
What must his future life be? was he brought
So low, who stood so lofty this Spring morn?
At length he said, "Best sleep now with my scorn,
And by to-morrow I devise some plain
Expedient!" So, he slept, nor woke again.
[Sidenote: Ending with what had possessed him.]
They found as much, those friends, when they returned
O'erflowing with the marvels they had learned
About Sordello's paradise, his roves
Among the hills and vales and plains and groves,
Wherein, no doubt, this lay was roughly cast,
Polished by slow degrees, completed last
To Eglamor's discomfiture and death.
Such form the chanters now, and, out of breath,
They lay the beaten man in his abode,
Naddo reciting that same luckless ode,
Doleful to hear. Sordello could explore
By means of it, however, one step more
In joy; and, mastering the round at length,
Learnt how to live in weakness as in strength,
When from his covert forth he stood, addressed
Eglamor, bade the tender ferns invest,
Primæval pines o'ercanopy his couch,
And, most of all, his fame—(shall I avouch
Eglamor heard it, dead though he might look,
And laughed as from his brow Sordello took
The crown, and laid on the bard's breast, and said
It was a crown, now, fit for poet's head?)
—Continue. Nor the prayer quite fruitless fell,
A plant they have, yielding a three-leaved bell
Which whitens at the heart ere noon, and ails
Till evening; evening gives it to her gales
To clear away with such forgotten things

As are an eyesore to the morn: this brings
Him to their mind, and hears his very name.
[Sidenote: Eglamor done with, Sordello begins.]
So much for Eglamor. My own month came;
'Twas a sunrise of blossoming and May.
Beneath a flowering laurel thicket lay
Sordello; each new sprinkle of white stars
That smell fainter of wine than Massic jars
Dug up at Baiæ, when the south wind shed
The ripest, made him happier; filleted
And robed the same, only a lute beside
Lay on the turf. Before him far and wide
The country stretched: Goito slept behind
—The castle and its covert, which confined
Him with his hopes and fears; so fain of old
To leave the story of his birth untold.
At intervals, 'spite the fantastic glow
Of his Apollo-life, a certain low
And wretched whisper, winding through the bliss,
Admonished, no such fortune could be his,
All was quite false and sure to fade one day:
The closelier drew he round him his array
Of brilliance to expel the truth. But when
A reason for his difference from men
Surprised him at the grave, he took no rest
While aught of that old life, superbly dressed
Down to its meanest incident, remained
A mystery: alas, they soon explained
Away Apollo! and the tale amounts
To this: when at Vicenza both her counts
[Sidenote: Who he really was, and why at Goito.]
Banished the Vivaresi kith and kin,
Those Maltraversi hung on Ecelin,
Reviled him as he followed; he for spite
Must fire their quarter, though that self-same night
Among the flames young Ecelin was born
Of Adelaide, there too, and barely torn
From the roused populace hard on the rear,
By a poor archer when his chieftain's fear
Grew high; into the thick Elcorte leapt,
Saved her, and died; no creature left except
His child to thank. And when the full escape
Was known—how men impaled from chine to nape
Unlucky Prata, all to pieces spurned
Bishop Pistore's concubines, and burned
Taurello's entire household, flesh and fell,
Missing the sweeter prey—such courage well
Might claim reward. The orphan, ever since,
Sordello, had been nurtured by his prince
Within a blind retreat where Adelaide—
(For, once this notable discovery made,

The past at every point was understood)
—Might harbor easily when times were rude,
When Azzo schemed for Palma, to retrieve
That pledge of Agnes Este—loth to leave
Mantua unguarded with a vigilant eye,
While there Taurello bode ambiguously—
He who could have no motive now to moil
For his own fortunes since their utter spoil—
As it were worth while yet (went the report)
To disengage himself from her. In short,
Apollo vanished; a mean youth, just named
His lady's minstrel, was to be proclaimed
—How shall I phrase it?—Monarch of the World!
[Sidenote: He, so little, would fain be so much:]
For, on the day when that array was furled
Forever, and in place of one a slave
To longings, wild indeed, but longings save
In dreams as wild, suppressed—one daring not
Assume the mastery such dreams allot,
Until a magical equipment, strength,
Grace, wisdom, decked him too,—he chose at length,
Content with unproved wits and failing frame,
In virtue of his simple will, to claim
That mastery, no less—to do his best
With means so limited, and let the rest
Go by,—the seal was set: never again
Sordello could in his own sight remain
[Sidenote: Leaves the dream he may be something,]
One of the many, one with hopes and cares
And interests nowise distinct from theirs,
Only peculiar in a thriveless store
Of fancies, which were fancies and no more;
Never again for him and for the crowd
A common law was challenged and allowed
If calmly reasoned of, howe'er denied
By a mad impulse nothing justified
Short of Apollo's presence. The divorce
Is clear: why needs Sordello square his course
By any known example? Men no more
Compete with him than tree and flower before.
Himself, inactive, yet is greater far
Than such as act, each stooping to his star,
Acquiring thence his function; he has gained
The same result with meaner mortals trained
To strength or beauty, moulded to express
Each the idea that rules him; since no less
He comprehends that function, but can still
Embrace the others, take of might his fill
With Richard as of grace with Palma, mix
Their qualities, or for a moment fix
On one; abiding free meantime, uncramped

By any partial organ, never stamped
Strong, and to strength turning all energies—
Wise, and restricted to becoming wise—
That is, he loves not, nor possesses One
Idea that, star-like over, lures him on
To its exclusive purpose. "Fortunate!
This flesh of mine ne'er strove to emulate
A soul so various—took no casual mould
Of the first fancy and, contracted, cold,
Clogged her forever—soul averse to change
As flesh: whereas flesh leaves soul free to range,
Remains itself a blank, east into shade,
Encumbers little, if it cannot aid.
[Sidenote: For the fact that he can do nothing,]
So, range, free soul!—who, by self-consciousness,
The last drop of all beauty dost express—
The grace of seeing grace, a quintessence
For thee: while for the world, that can dispense
Wonder on men who, themselves, wonder—make
A shift to love at second-hand, and take
For idols those who do but idolize,
Themselves,—the world that counts men strong or wise,
Who, themselves, court strength, wisdom,—it shall bow
Surely in unexampled worship now,
Discerning me!"—
(Dear monarch, I beseech,
Notice how lamentably wide a breach
Is here: discovering this, discover too
What our poor world has possibly to do
With it! As pigmy natures as you please—
So much the better for you; take your ease,
Look on, and laugh; style yourself God alone;
Strangle some day with a cross olive-stone!
All that is right enough: but why want us
To know that you yourself know thus and thus?)
"The world shall bow to me conceiving all
Man's life, who see its blisses, great and small,
Afar—not tasting any; no machine
To exercise my utmost will is mine:
Be mine mere consciousness! Let men perceive
What I could do, a mastery believe,
Asserted and established to the throng
By their selected evidence of song
Which now shall prove, whate'er they are, or seek
To be, I am—whose words, not actions speak,
Who change no standards of perfection, vex
With no strange forms created to perplex,
But just perform their bidding and no more,
At their own satiating-point give o'er,
While each shall love in me the love that leads
His soul to power's perfection." Song, not deeds,

(For we get tired) was chosen. Fate would brook
Mankind no other organ; he would look
For not another channel to dispense
His own volition by, receive men's sense
Of its supremacy—would live content,
Obstructed else, with merely verse for vent.
[Sidenote: Yet is able to imagine everything,]
Nor should, for instance, strength an outlet seek
And, striving, be admired; nor grace bespeak
Wonder, displayed in gracious attitudes;
Nor wisdom, poured forth, change unseemly moods:
But he would give and take on song's one point.
Like some huge throbbing stone that, poised a-joint,
Sounds, to affect on its basaltic bed,
Must sue in just one accent; tempests shed
Thunder, and raves the windstorm: only let
That key by any little noise be set—
The far benighted hunter's halloo pitch
On that, the hungry curlew chance to scritch
Or serpent hiss it, rustling through the rift,
However loud, however low—all lift
The groaning monster, stricken to the heart.
Lo ye, the world's concernment, for its part,
[Sidenote: If the world esteem this equivalent.]
And this, for his, will hardly interfere!
Its businesses in blood and blaze this year
But while the hour away—a pastime slight
Till he shall step upon the platform: right!
And, now thus much is settled, cast in rough,
Proved feasible, be counselled! thought enough,—
Slumber, Sordello! any day will serve:
Were it a less digested plan! how swerve
To-morrow? Meanwhile eat these sun-dried grapes,
And watch the soaring hawk there! Life escapes
Merrily thus.

He thoroughly read o'er
His truchman Naddo's missive six times more,
Praying him visit Mantua and supply
A famished world.

The evening star was high
When he reached Mantua, but his fame arrived
Before him: friends applauded, foes connived,
And Naddo looked an angel, and the rest
Angels, and all these angels would he blest
Supremely by a song—the thrice-renowned
Goito-manufacture. Then he found
(Casting about to satisfy the crowd)
[Sidenote: He has loved song's results, not song;]
That happy vehicle, so late allowed,

A sore annoyance; 't was the song's effect
He cared for, scarce the song itself: reflect!
In the past life, what might be singing's use?
Just to delight his Delians, whose profuse
Praise, not the toilsome process which procured
That praise, enticed Apollo: dreams abjured,
No overleaping means for ends—take both
For granted or take neither! I am loth
To say the rhymes at last were Eglamor's;
But Naddo, chuckling, bade competitors
Go pine; "the master certes meant to waste
No effort, cautiously had probed the taste
He 'd please anon: true bard, in short, disturb
His title if they could; nor spur nor curb,
Fancy nor reason, wanting in him; whence
The staple of his verses, common sense:
He built on man's broad nature—gift of gifts,
That power to build! The world contented shifts
With counterfeits enough, a dreary sort
Of warriors, statesmen, ere it can extort
Its poet-soul—that 's, after all, a freak
(The having eyes to see and tongue to speak)
With our herd's stupid sterling happiness
So plainly incompatible that—yes—
Yes—should a son of his improve the breed
And turn out poet, he were cursed indeed!"
"Well, there 's Goito and its woods anon,
If the worst happen; best go stoutly on
Now!" thought Sordello.
[Sidenote: So, must effect this to obtain those.]

Ay, and goes on yet!
You pother with your glossaries to get
A notion of the Troubadour's intent
In rondel, tenzon, virlai, or sirvent—
Much as you study arras how to twirl
His angelot, plaything of page and girl
Once; but you surely reach, at last,—or, no!
Never quite reach what struck the people so,
As from the welter of their time he drew
Its elements successively to view,
Followed all actions backward on their course,
And catching up, unmingled at the source,
Such a strength, such a weakness, added then
A touch or two, and turned them into men.
Virtue took form, nor vice refused a shape;
Here heaven opened, there was hell agape,
As Saint this simpered past in sanctity,
Sinner the other flared portentous by
A greedy people. Then why stop, surprised
At his success? The scheme was realized

Too suddenly in one respect: a crowd
Praising, eyes quick to see, and lips as loud
To speak, delicious homage to receive,
The woman's breath to feel upon his sleeve,
Who said, "But Anafest—why asks he less
Than Lucio, in your verses? how confess,
It seemed too much but yestereve!"—the youth,
Who bade him earnestly, "Avow the truth!
You love Bianca, surely, from your song;
I knew I was unworthy!"—soft or strong,
In poured such tributes ere he had arranged
Ethereal ways to take them, sorted, changed,
Digested. Courted thus at unawares,
In spite of his pretensions and his cares,
He caught himself shamefully hankering
After the obvious petty joys that spring
From true life, fain relinquish pedestal
[Sidenote: He succeeds a little, but fails more;]
And condescend with pleasures—one and all
To be renounced, no doubt; for, thus to chain
Himself to single joys and so refrain
From tasting their quintessence, frustrates, sure,
His prime design; each joy must he abjure
Even for love of it.

He laughed: what sage
But perishes if from his magic page
He look because, at the first line, a proof
'T was heard salutes him from the cavern roof?
"On! Give yourself, excluding aught beside,
To the day's task; compel your slave provide
Its utmost at the soonest; turn the leaf
Thoroughly conned. These lays of yours, in brief—
Cannot men hear, now, something better?—fly
A pitch beyond this unreal pageantry
Of essences? the period sure has ceased
For such: present us with ourselves, at least,
Not portions of ourselves, mere loves and hates
Made flesh: wait not!"
[Sidenote: Tries again, is no better satisfied,]

Awhile the poet waits
However. The first trial was enough:
He left imagining, to try the stuff
That held the imaged thing, and, let it writhe
Never so fiercely, scarce allowed a tithe
To reach the light—his Language. How he sought
The cause, conceived a cure, and slow re-wrought
That Language,—welding words into the crude
Mass from the new speech round him, till a rude
Armor was hammered out, in time to be

Approved beyond the Roman panoply
Melted to make it,—boots not. This obtained
With some ado, no obstacle remained
To using it; accordingly he took
An action with its actors, quite forsook
Himself to live in each, returned anon
With the result—a creature, and, by one
And one, proceeded leisurely to equip
Its limbs in harness of his workmanship.
"Accomplished! Listen, Mantuans!" Fond essay!
Piece after piece that armor broke away,
Because perceptions whole, like that he sought
To clothe, reject so pure a work of thought
As language: thought may take perception's place
But hardly co-exist in any case,
Being its mere presentment—of the whole
By parts, the simultaneous and the sole
By the successive and the many. Lacks
The crowd perception? painfully it tacks
Thought to thought, which Sordello, needing such,
Has rent perception into: it 's to clutch
And reconstruct—his office to diffuse,
Destroy: as hard, then, to obtain a Muse
As to become Apollo. "For the rest,
E'en if some wondrous vehicle expressed
The whole dream, what impertinence in me
So to express it, who myself can be
The dream! nor, on the other hand, are those
I sing to, over-likely to suppose
[Sidenote: And declines from the ideal of song.]
A higher than the highest I present
Now, which they praise already: be content
Both parties, rather—they with the old verse,
And I with the old praise—far go, fare worse!"
A few adhering rivets loosed, upsprings
The angel, sparkles off his mail, which rings
Whirled from each delicatest limb it warps,
So might Apollo from the sudden corpse
Of Hyacinth have cast his luckless quoits.
He set to celebrating the exploits
Of Montfort o'er the Mountaineers.

Then came
The world's revenge: their pleasure, now his aim
Merely,—what was it? "Not to play the fool
So much as learn our lesson in your school!"
Replied the world. He found that, every time
He gained applause by any ballad-rhyme,
His auditory recognized no jot
As he intended, and, mistaking not
Him for his meanest hero, ne'er was dunce

Sufficient to believe him—all, at once.
His will ... conceive it caring for his will!
—Mantuans, the main of them, admiring still
How a mere singer, ugly, stunted, weak,
Had Montfort at completely (so to speak)
His fingers' ends; while past the praise-tide swept
To Montfort, either's share distinctly kept:
The true meed for true merit!—his abates
[Sidenote: What is the world's recognition worth?]
Into a sort he most repudiates,
And on them angrily he turns. Who were
The Mantuans, after all, that he should care
About their recognition, ay or no?
In spite of the convention months ago,
(Why blink the truth?) was not he forced to help
This same ungrateful audience, every whelp
Of Naddo's litter, make them pass for peers
With the bright band of old Goito years,
As erst he toiled for flower or tree? Why, there
Sat Palma! Adelaide's funereal hair
Ennobled the next corner. Ay, he strewed
A fairy dust upon that multitude,
Although he feigned to take them by themselves;
His giants dignified those puny elves,
Sublime their faint applause. In short, he found
Himself still footing a delusive round,
Remote as ever from the self-display
He meant to compass, hampered every way
By what he hoped assistance. Wherefore then
Continue, make believe to find in men
A use he found not?

Weeks, months, years went by,
And lo, Sordello vanished utterly,
Sundered in twain; each spectral part at strife
With each; one jarred against another life;
[Sidenote: How, poet no longer in unity with man,]
The Poet thwarting hopelessly the Man,
Who, fooled no longer, free in fancy ran
Here, there,—let slip no opportunities
As pitiful, forsooth, beside the prize
To drop on him some no-time and acquit
His constant faith (the Poet-half's to wit—
That waiving any compromise between
No joy and all joy kept the hunger keen
Beyond most methods)—of incurring scoff
From the Man-portion—not to be put off
With self-reflectings by the Poet's scheme,
Though ne'er so bright. Who sauntered forth in dream,
Dressed anyhow, nor waited mystic frames,
Immeasurable gifts, astounding claims,

But just his sorry self?—who yet might be
Sorrier for aught he in reality
Achieved, so pinioned Man 's the Poet-part,
Fondling, in turn of fancy, verse; the Art
Developing his soul a thousand ways—
Potent, by its assistance, to amaze
The multitude with majesties, convince
Each sort of nature, that the nature's prince
Accosted it. Language, the makeshift, grew
Into a bravest of expedients, too;
Apollo, seemed it now, perverse had thrown
Quiver and bow away, the lyre alone
Sufficed. While, out of dream, his day's work went
To tune a crazy tenzon or sirvent—
So hampered him the Man-part, thrust to judge
Between the bard and the bard's audience, grudge
A minute's toil that missed its due reward!
But the complete Sordello, Man and Bard,

[Sidenote: The whole visible Sordello goes wrong]

John's cloud-girt angel, this foot on the land,
That on the sea, with, open in his hand,
A bitter-sweetling of a book—was gone.
Then, if internal straggles to be one
Which frittered him incessantly piecemeal,
Referred, ne'er so obliquely, to the real
Intruding Mantuans! ever with some call
To action while he pondered, once for all,
Which looked the easier effort—to pursue
This course, still leap o'er paltry joys, yearn through
The present ill-appreciated stage
Of self-revealment, and compel the age
Know him; or else, forswearing bard-craft, wake
From out his lethargy and nobly shake
Off timid habits of denial, mix
With men, enjoy like men. Ere he could fix
On aught, in rushed the Mantuans; much they cared
For his perplexity! Thus unprepared,
The obvious if not only shelter lay

[Sidenote: With those too hard for half of him,]

In deeds, the dull conventions of his day
Prescribed the like of him: why not be glad
'T is settled Palma's minstrel, good or bad,
Submits to this and that established rule?
Let Vidal change, or any other fool,
His murrey-colored robe for filamot,
And crop his hair; too skin-deep, is it not,
Such vigor? Then, a sorrow to the heart,
His talk! Whatever topics they might start
Had to be groped for in his consciousness
Straight, and as straight delivered them by guess.
Only obliged to ask himself, "What was,"

A speedy answer followed; but, alas,
One of God's large ones, tardy to condense
Itself into a period; answers whence
A tangle of conclusions must be stripped
At any risk ere, trim to pattern clipped,
They matched rare specimens the Mantuan flock
Regaled him with, each talker from his stock
Of sorted-o'er opinions, every stage,
Juicy in youth or desiccate with age,
Fruits like the fig-tree's, rathe-ripe, rotten-rich,
Sweet-sour, all tastes to take: a practice which
He too had not impossibly attained,
Once either of those fancy-flights restrained;
(For, at conjecture how might words appear
To others, playing there what happened here,
And occupied abroad by what he spurned
At home, 't was slipped, the occasion he returned
To seize:) he 'd strike that lyre adroitly—speech,
Would but a twenty-cubit plectre reach;
A clever hand, consummate instrument,
Were both brought close; each excellency went
For nothing, else. The question Naddo asked,
Had just a lifetime moderately tasked
To answer, Naddo's fashion. More disgust
[Sidenote: Of whom he is also too contemptuous.]
And more: why move his soul, since move it must
At minute's notice or as good it failed
To move at all? The end was, he retailed
Some ready-made opinion, put to use
This quip, that maxim, ventured reproduce
Gestures and tones—at any folly caught
Serving to finish with, nor too much sought
If false or true 't was spoken; praise and blame
Of what he said grew pretty nigh the same
—Meantime awards to meantime acts: his soul,
Unequal to the compassing a whole,
Saw, in a tenth part, less and less to strive
About. And as for men in turn ... contrive
Who could to take eternal interest
In them, so hate the worst, so love the best!
Though, in pursuance of his passive plan,
He hailed, decried, the proper way.

As Man
So figured he; and how as Poet? Verse
Came only not to a stand-still. The worse,
That his poor piece of daily work to do
Was, not sink under any rivals; who
[Sidenote: He pleases neither himself nor them:]
Loudly and long enough, without these qualms,
Turned, from Bocafoli's stark-naked psalms,

To Plara's sonnets spoilt by toying with,
"As knops that stud some almug to the pith
Prickèd for gum, wry thence, and crinklèd worse
Than pursèd eyelids of a river-horse
Sunning himself o' the slime when whirrs the breeze"—
Gad-fly, that is. He might compete with these!
But—but—

"Observe a pompion-twine afloat;
Pluck me one cup from off the castle-moat!
[Sidenote: Which the best judges account for.]
Along with cup you raise leaf, stalk and root,
The entire surface of the pool to boot.
So could I pluck a cup, put in one song
A single sight, did not my hand, too strong,
Twitch in the least the root-strings of the whole.
How should externals satisfy my soul?"
"Why that 's precise the error Squarcialupe"
(Hazarded Naddo) "finds; 'the man can't stoop
To sing us out,' quoth he, 'a mere romance;
He 'd fain do better than the best, enhance
The subjects' rarity, work problems out
Therewith.' Now, you 're a bard, a bard past doubt,
And no philosopher; why introduce
Crotchets like these? fine, surely, but no use
In poetry—which still must be, to strike,
Based upon common sense; there 's nothing like
Appealing to our nature! what beside
Was your first poetry? No tricks were tried
In that, no hollow thrills, affected throes!
'The man,' said we, 'tells his own joys and woes:
We 'll trust him.' Would you have your songs endure?
Build on the human heart!—why, to be sure
Yours is one sort of heart—but I mean theirs,
Ours, every one's, the healthy heart one cares
To build on! Central peace, mother of strength,
That 's father of ... nay, go yourself that length,
Ask those calm-hearted doers what they do
When they have got their calm! And is it true,
Fire rankles at the heart of every globe?
Perhaps. But these are matters one may probe
Too deeply for poetic purposes:
Rather select a theory that ... yes,
Laugh! what does that prove?—stations you midway
And saves some little o'er-refining. Nay,
That 's rank injustice done me! I restrict
The poet? Don't I hold the poet picked
Out of a host of warriors, statesmen ... did
I tell you? Very like! As well you hid
That sense of power, you have! True bards believe
All able to achieve what they achieve—

That is, just nothing—in one point abide
Profounder simpletons than all beside.
Oh, ay! The knowledge that you are a bard
Must constitute your prime, nay sole, reward!"
So prattled Naddo, busiest of the tribe
Of genius-haunters—how shall I describe
What grubs or nips or rubs or rips—your louse
For love, your flea for hate, magnanimous,
[Sidenote: Their criticisms give small comfort:]
Malignant, Pappacoda, Tagliafer,
Picking a sustenance from wear and tear
By implements it sedulous employs
To undertake, lay down, mete out, o'er-toise
Sordello? Fifty creepers to elude
At once! They settled stanchly: shame ensued:
Behold the monarch of mankind succumb
To the last fool who turned him round his thumb,
As Naddo styled it! 'T was not worth oppose
The matter of a moment, gainsay those
He aimed at getting rid of; better think
Their thoughts and speak their speech, secure to slink
Back expeditiously to his safe place,
And chew the cud—what he and what his race
Were really, each of them. Yet even this
Conformity was partial. He would miss
Some point, brought into contact with them ere
Assured in what small segment of the sphere
Of his existence they attended him;
Whence blunders, falsehoods rectified—a grim
List—slur it over! How? If dreams were tried,
His will swayed sicklily from side to side,
Nor merely neutralized his waking act
But tended e'en in fancy to distract
The intermediate will, the choice of means.
He lost the art of dreaming: Mantuan scenes
Supplied a baron, say, he sang before,
Handsomely reckless, full to running o'er
Of gallantries; "abjure the soul, content
With body, therefore!" Scarcely had he bent
Himself in dream thus low, when matter fast
Cried out, he found, for spirit to contrast
And task it duly; by advances slight,
The simple stuff becoming composite,
Count Lori grew Apollo—best recall
His fancy! Then would some rough peasant-Paul,
Like those old Ecelin confers with, glance
His gay apparel o'er; that countenance
Gathered his shattered fancies into one,
And, body clean abolished, soul alone
Sufficed the gray Paulieian: by and by,
[Sidenote: And his own degradation is complete.]

To balance the ethereality,
Passions were needed; foiled he sank again.
Meanwhile the world rejoiced ('t is time explain)
Because a sudden sickness set it free
From Adelaide. Missing the mother-bee,
Her mountain-hive Romano swarmed; at once
A rustle-forth of daughters and of sons
Blackened the valley. "I am sick too, old,
Half-crazed I think; what good 's the Kaiser's gold
To such an one? God help me! for I catch
My children's greedy sparkling eyes at watch—
'He bears that double breastplate on,' they say,
'So many minutes less than yesterday!'
Beside, Monk Hilary is on his knees
Now, sworn to kneel and pray till God shall please
Exact a punishment for many things
You know, and some you never knew; which brings
To memory, Azzo's sister Beatrix
And Richard's Giglia are my Alberic's
And Ecelin's betrothed; the Count himself
Must get my Palma: Ghibellin and Guelf
Mean to embrace each other." So began
[Sidenote: Adelaide's death: what happens on it:]
Romano's missive to his fighting man
Taurello—on the Tuscan's death, away
With Friedrich sworn to sail from Naples' bay
Next month for Syria. Never thunder-clap
Out of Vesuvius' throat, like this mishap
Startled him. "That accursed Vicenza! I
Absent, and she selects this time to die!
Ho, fellows, for Vicenza!" Half a score
Of horses ridden dead, he stood before
Romano in his reeking spurs: too late—
"Boniface urged me, Este could not wait,"
The chieftain stammered; "let me die in peace—
Forget me! Was it I who craved increase
Of rule? Do you and Friedrich plot your worst
Against the Father: as you found me first
So leave me now. Forgive me! Palma, sure,
Is at Goito still. Retain that lure—
Only be pacified!"

The country rung
With such a piece of news: on every tongue,
How Ecelin's great servant, congeed off,
Had done a long day's service, so, might doff
The green and yellow, and recover breath
At Mantua, whither,—since Retrude's death,
(The girlish slip of a Sicilian bride
From Otho's house, he carried to reside
At Mantua till the Ferrarese should pile

A structure worthy her imperial style,
The gardens raise, the statues there enshrine,
She never lived to see)—although his line
Was ancient in her archives and she took
A pride in him, that city, nor forsook
Her child when he forsook himself and spent
A prowess on Romano surely meant
For his own growth—whither he ne'er resorts
If wholly satisfied (to trust reports)
With Ecelin. So, forward in a trice
Were shows to greet him. "Take a friend's advice,"
Quoth Naddo to Sordello, "nor be rash
Because your rivals (nothing can abash
Some folks) demur that we pronounced you best
To sound the great man's welcome; 't is a test,
Remember! Strojavacca looks asquint,
The rough fat sloven; and there 's plenty hint
Your pinions have received of late a shock—
Outsoar them, cobswan of the silver flock!
[Sidenote: And a trouble it occasions Sordello.]
Sing well!" A signal wonder, song 's no whit
Facilitated.

Fast the minutes flit;
Another day, Sordello finds, will bring
The soldier, and he cannot choose but sing;
So, a last shift, quits Mantua—slow, alone:
Out of that aching brain, a very stone,
Song must be struck. What occupies that front?
Just how he was more awkward than his wont
The night before, when Naddo, who had seen
Taurello on his progress, praised the mien
For dignity no crosses could affect—
Such was a joy, and might not he detect
A satisfaction if established joys
Were proved imposture? Poetry annoys
Its utmost: wherefore fret? Verses may come
Or keep away! And thus he wandered, dumb
Till evening, when he paused, thoroughly spent,
On a blind hill-top: down the gorge he went,
Yielding himself up as to an embrace.
The moon came out; like features of a face,
A querulous fraternity of pines,
Sad blackthorn clumps, leafless and grovelling vines
Also came out, made gradually up
The picture; 't was Goito's mountain-cup
And castle. He had dropped through one defile
He never dared explore, the Chief erewhile
[Sidenote: He chances upon his old environment,]
Had vanished by. Back rushed the dream, enwrapped
Him wholly. 'T was Apollo now they lapped,

Those mountains, not a pettish minstrel meant
To wear his soul away in discontent,
Brooding on fortune's malice. Heart and brain
Swelled; he expanded to himself again,
As some thin seedling spice-tree starved and frail,
Pushing between cat's head and ibis' tail
Crusted into the porphyry pavement smooth,
—Suffered remain just as it sprung, to soothe
The Soldan's pining daughter, never yet
Well in her chilly green-glazed minaret,—
When rooted up, the sunny day she died,
And flung into the common court beside
Its parent tree. Come home, Sordello! Soon
Was he low muttering, beneath the moon,
Of sorrow saved, of quiet evermore,—
Since from the purpose, he maintained before,
Only resulted wailing and hot tears.
[Sidenote: Sees but failure in all done since,]
Ah, the slim castle! dwindled of late years,
But more mysterious; gone to ruin—trails
Of vine through every loop-hole. Naught avails
The night as, torch in hand, he must explore
The maple chamber: did I say, its floor
Was made of intersecting cedar beams?
Worn now with gaps so large, there blew cold streams
Of air quite from the dungeon; lay your ear
Close and 't is like, one after one, you hear
In the blind darkness water drop. The nests
And nooks retain their long ranged vesture-chests
Empty and smelling of the iris root
The Tuscan grated o'er them to recruit .
Her wasted wits. Palma was gone that day,
Said the remaining women. Last, he lay
Beside the Carian group reserved and still.
The Body, the Machine for Acting Will,
Had been at the commencement proved unfit;
That for Demonstrating, Reflecting it,
Mankind—no fitter: was the Will Itself
In fault?

His forehead pressed the moonlit shelf
Beside the youngest marble maid awhile;
Then, raising it, he thought, with a long smile,
[Sidenote: and resolves to desist from the like.]
"I shall be king again!" as he withdrew
The envied scarf; into the font he threw
His crown.

Next day, no poet! "Wherefore?" asked
Taurello, when the dance of Jongleurs, masked
As devils, ended; "don't a song come next?"

The master of the pageant looked perplexed
Till Naddo's whisper came to his relief.
"His Highness knew what poets were: in brief,
Had not the tetchy race prescriptive right
To peevishness, caprice? or, call it spite,
One must receive their nature in its length
And breadth, expect the weakness with the strength!"
—So phrasing, till, his stock of phrases spent,
The easy-natured soldier smiled assent,
Settled his portly person, smoothed his chin,
And nodded that the bull-bait might begin.

BOOK THE THIRD

And the font took them: let our laurels lie!
Braid moonfern now with mystic trifoly
Because once more Goito gets, once more,
Sordello to itself! A dream is o'er,
And the suspended life begins anew;
Quiet those throbbing temples, then, subdue
[Sidenote: Nature may triumph therefore;]
That cheek's distortion! Nature's strict embrace,
Putting aside the past, shall soon efface
Its print as well—factitious humors grown
Over the true—loves, hatreds not his own—
And turn him pure as some forgotten vest
Woven of painted byssus, silkiest
Tufting the Tyrrhene whelk's pearl-sheeted lip,
Left welter where a trireme let it slip
I' the sea, and vexed a satrap; so the stain
O' the world forsakes Sordello, with its pain,
Its pleasure: how the tinct loosening escapes,
Cloud after cloud! Mantua's familiar shapes
Die, fair and foul die, fading as they flit,
Men, women, and the pathos and the wit,
Wise speech and foolish, deeds to smile or sigh
For, good, bad, seemly or ignoble, die.
The last face glances through the eglantines,
The last voice murmurs, 'twixt the blossomed vines,
Of Men, of that machine supplied by thought
To compass self-perception with, he sought
By forcing half himself—an insane pulse
Of a god's blood, on clay it could convulse,
Never transmute—on human sights and sounds,
To watch the other half with; irksome bounds
It ebbs from to its source, a fountain sealed
Forever. Better sure be unrevealed
Than part revealed: Sordello well or ill
Is finished: then what further use of Will,

Point in the prime idea not realized,
An oversight? inordinately prized,
No less, and pampered with enough of each
Delight to prove the whole above its reach.
"To need become all natures, yet retain
The law of my own nature—to remain
Myself, yet yearn ... as if that chestnut, think,
Should yearn for this first larch-bloom crisp and pink,
Or those pale fragrant tears where zephyrs stanch
March wounds along the fretted pine-tree branch!
Will and the means to show will, great and small,
Material, spiritual,—abjure them all
Save any so distinct, they may be left
To amuse, not tempt become! and, thus bereft,
Just as I first was fashioned would I be!
Nor, moon, is it Apollo now, but me
[Sidenote: For her son, lately alive, dies again,]
Thou visitest to comfort and befriend!
Swim thou into my heart, and there an end,
Since I possess thee!—nay, thus shut mine eyes
And know, quite know, by this heart's fall and rise,
When thou dost bury thee in clouds, and when
Out-standest: wherefore practise upon men
To make that plainer to myself?"

Slide here
Over a sweet and solitary year
Wasted; or simply notice change in him—
How eyes, once with exploring bright, grew dim
And satiate with receiving. Some distress
Was caused, too, by a sort of consciousness
Under the imbecility,—naught kept
That down; he slept, but was aware he slept,
So, frustrated: as who brainsick made pact
Erst with the overhanging cataract
To deafen him, yet still distinguished plain
His own blood's measured clicking at his brain.
To finish. One declining Autumn day—
Few birds about the heaven chill and gray,
No wind that cared trouble the tacit woods—
He sauntered home complacently, their moods
According, his and nature's. Every spark
[Sidenote: Was found and is lost.]
Of Mantua life was trodden out; so dark
The embers, that the Troubadour, who sung
Hundreds of songs, forgot, its trick his tongue,
Its craft his brain, how either brought to pass
Singing at all; that faculty might class
With any of Apollo's now. The year
Began to find its early promise sere
As well. Thus beauty vanishes; thus stone

Outlingers flesh: nature's and his youth gone,
They left the world to you, and wished you joy,
When, stopping his benevolent employ,
A presage shuddered through the welkin; harsh
The earth's remonstrance followed. 'T was the marsh
Gone of a sudden. Mincio, in its place,
Laughed, a broad water, in next morning's face,
And, where the mists broke up immense and white
I' the steady wind, burned like a spilth of light
Out of the crashing of a myriad stars.
And here was nature, bound by the same bars
Of fate with him!
[Sidenote: But nature is one thing, man another—]

"No! youth once gone is gone:
Deeds let escape are never to be done.
Leaf-fall and grass-spring for the year; for us—
Oh forfeit I unalterably thus
My chance? nor two lives wait me, this to spend,
Learning save that? Nature has time, may mend
Mistake, she knows occasion will recur;
Landslip or seabreach, how affects it her
With her magnificent resources?—I
Must perish once and perish utterly.
Not any strollings now at even-close
Down the field-path, Sordello! by thorn-rows
Alive with lamp-flies, swimming spots of fire
And dew, outlining the black cypress' spire
She waits you at, Elys, who heard you first
Woo her, the snow-month through, but ere she durst
Answer 't was April. Linden-flower-time-long
Her eyes were on the ground; 't is July, strong
Now; and because white dust-clouds overwhelm
The woodside, here or by the village elm
That holds the moon, she meets you, somewhat pale,
But letting you lift up her coarse flax veil
And whisper (the damp little hand in yours)
Of love, heart's love, your heart's love that endures
Till death. Tush! No mad mixing with the rout
Of haggard ribalds wandering about
The hot torchlit wine-scented island-house
Where Friedrich holds his wickedest carouse,
Parading,—to the gay Palermitans,
Soft Messinese, dusk Saracenic clans
[Sidenote: Having multifarious sympathies,]
Nuocera holds,—those tall grave dazzling Norse,
High-cheeked, lank-haired, toothed whiter than the morse,
Queens of the caves of jet stalactites,
He sent his barks to fetch through icy seas,
The blind night seas without a saving star,
And here in snowy birdskin robes they are,

Sordello!—here, mollitious alcoves gilt
Superb as Byzant domes that devils built!
—Ah, Byzant, there again! no chance to go
Ever like august cheery Dandolo,
Worshipping hearts about him for a wall,
Conducted, blind eyes, hundred years and all,
Through vanquished Byzant where friends note for him
What pillar, marble massive, sardius slim,
'T were fittest he transport to Venice' Square—
Flattered and promised life to touch them there
Soon, by those fervid sons of senators!
No more lifes, deaths, loves, hatreds, peaces, wars!
Ah, fragments of a whole ordained to be,
Points in the life I waited! what are ye
But roundels of a ladder which appeared
Awhile the very platform it was reared
To lift me on?—that happiness I find
Proofs of my faith in, even in the blind
Instinct which bade forego you all unless
Ye led me past yourselves. Ay, happiness
[Sidenote: He may neither renounce nor satisfy;]
Awaited me; the way life should be used
Was to acquire, and deeds like you conduced
To teach it by a self-revealment, deemed
Life's very use, so long! Whatever seemed
Progress to that, was pleasure; aught that stayed
My reaching it—no pleasure. I have laid
The ladder down; I climb not; still, aloft
The platform stretches! Blisses strong and soft,
I dared not entertain, elude me; yet
Never of what they promised could I get
A glimpse till now! The common sort, the crowd,
Exist, perceive; with Being are endowed,
However slight, distinct from what they See,
However bounded; Happiness must be,
To feed the first by gleanings from the last,
Attain its qualities, and slow or fast
Become what they behold; such peace-in-strife
By transmutation, is the Use of Life,
The Alien turning Native to the soul
Or body—which instructs me; I am whole
There and demand a Palma; had the world
Been from my soul to a like distance hurled,
'T were Happiness to make it one with me:
Whereas I must, ere I begin to Be,
Include a world, in flesh, I comprehend
In spirit now; and this done, what 's to blend
With? Naught is Alien in the world—my Will
[Sidenote: In the process to which is pleasure,]
Owns all already; yet can turn it—still
Less—Native, since my Means to correspond

With Will are so unworthy, 't was my bond
To tread the very joys that tantalize
Most now, into a grave, never to rise.
I die then! Will the rest agree to die?
Next Age or no? Shall its Sordello try
Clue after clue, and catch at last the clue
I miss?—that 's underneath my finger too,
Twice, thrice a day, perhaps,—some yearning traced
Deeper, some petty consequence embraced
Closer! Why fled I Mantua, then?—complained
So much my Will was fettered, yet remained
Content within a tether half the range
I could assign it?—able to exchange
My ignorance (I felt) for knowledge, and
Idle because I could thus understand—
Could e'en have penetrated to its core
Our mortal mystery, yet—fool—forbore,
Preferred elaborating in the dark
My casual stuff, by any wretched spark
Born of my predecessors, though one stroke
Of mine had brought the flame forth! Mantua's yoke,
My minstrel's-trade, was to behold mankind,—
My own concern was just to bring my mind
Behold, just extricate, for my acquist,
Each object suffered stifle in the mist
Which hazard, custom, blindness interpose
Betwixt things and myself."

Whereat he rose.
The level wind carried above the firs
Clouds, the irrevocable travellers,
Onward.

"Pushed thus into a drowsy copse,
Arms twine about my neck, each eyelid drops
Under a humid finger; while there fleets,
Outside the screen, a pageant time repeats
Never again! To be deposed, immured
[Sidenote: While renunciation ensures despair.]
Clandestinely—still petted, still assured
To govern were fatiguing work—the Sight
Fleeting meanwhile! 'T is noontide: wreak ere night
Somehow my will upon it, rather! Slake
This thirst somehow, the poorest impress take
That serves! A blasted bud displays you, torn,
Faint rudiments of the full flower unborn;
But who divines what glory coats o'erclasp
Of the bulb dormant in the mummy's grasp
Taurello sent?" ...

"Taurello? Palma sent

Your Trouvere," (Naddo interposing leant
Over the lost bard's shoulder)—"and, believe,
You cannot more reluctantly receive
Than I pronounce her message: we depart
Together. What avail a poet's heart
Verona's pomps and gauds? five blades of grass
Suffice him. News? Why, where your marish was,
On its mud-banks smoke rises after smoke
I' the valley, like a spout of hell new-broke.
Oh, the world's tidings! small your thanks, I guess,
For them. The father of our Patroness
Has played Taurello an astounding trick,
Parts between Ecelin and Alberic
His wealth and goes into a convent: both
Wed Guelfs: the Count and Palma plighted troth
A week since at Verona: and they want
You doubtless to contrive the marriage-chant
Ere Richard storms Ferrara." Then was told
The tale from the beginning—how, made bold
By Salinguerra's absence, Guelfs had burned
And pillaged till he unawares returned
To take revenge: how Azzo and his friend
Were doing their endeavor, how the end
O' the siege was nigh, and how the Count, released
From further care, would with his marriage-feast
[Sidenote: There is yet a way of escaping this;]
Inaugurate a new and better rule,
Absorbing thus Romano.

"Shall I school
My master," added Naddo, "and suggest
How you may clothe in a poetic vest
These doings, at Verona? Your response
To Palma! Wherefore jest? 'Depart at once?'
A good resolve! In truth, I hardly hoped
So prompt an acquiescence. Have you groped
Out wisdom in the wilds here?—Thoughts may be
Over-poetical for poetry.
Pearl-white, you poets liken Palma's neck;
And yet what spoils an orient like some speck
Of genuine white, turning its own white gray?
You take me? Curse the cicala!"

One more day,
One eve—appears Verona! Many a group,
(You mind) instructed of the osprey's swoop
On lynx and ounce, was gathering—Christendom
Sure to receive, whate'er the end was, from
The evening's purpose cheer or detriment,
Since Friedrich only waited some event
Like this, of Ghibellins establishing

Themselves within Ferrara, ere, as King
Of Lombardy, he 'd glad descend there, wage
Old warfare with the Pontiff, disengage
His barons from the burghers, and restore
The rule of Charlemagne, broken of yore
By Hildebrand.
[Sidenote: Which he now takes by obeying Palma:]

I' the palace, each by each,
Sordello sat and Palma: little speech
At first in that dim closet, face with face
(Despite the tumult in the market-place)
Exchanging quick low laughters: now would rush
Word upon word to meet a sudden flush,
A look left off, a shifting lips' surmise—
But for the most part their two histories
[Sidenote: Who thereupon becomes his associate.]
Ran best through the locked fingers and linked arms.
And so the night flew on with its alarms
Till in burst one of Palma's retinue;
"Now, Lady!" gasped he. Then arose the two
And leaned into Verona's air, dead-still.
A balcony lay black beneath until
Out, 'mid a gush of torchfire, gray-haired men
Came on it and harangued the people: then
Sea-like that people surging to and fro
Shouted, "Hale forth the carroch—trumpets, ho,
A flourish! Run it in the ancient grooves!
Back from the bell! Hammer—that whom behooves
May hear the League is up! Peal—learn who list,
Verona means not first of towns break tryst
To-morrow with the League!"

Enough. Now turn—
Over the eastern cypresses: discern!
Is any beacon set a-glimmer?

Rang
The air with shouts that overpowered the clang
Of the incessant carroch, even: "Haste—
The candle 's at the gateway! ere it waste,
Each soldier stand beside it, armed to march
With Tiso Sampier through the eastern arch!"
Ferrara 's succored, Palma!

Once again
They sat together; some strange thing in train
To say, so difficult was Palma's place
In taking, with a coy fastidious grace
Like the bird's flutter ere it fix and feed.
But when she felt she held her friend indeed

Safe, she threw back her curls, began implant
Her lessons; telling of another want
[Sidenote: As her own history will account for,]
Goito's quiet nourished than his own;
Palma—to serve him—to be served, alone
Importing; Agnes' milk so neutralized
The blood of Ecelin. Nor be surprised
If, while Sordello fain had captive led
Nature, in dream was Palma subjected
To some out-soul, which dawned not though she pined
Delaying till its advent, heart and mind,
Their life. "How dared I let expand the force
Within me, till some out-soul, whose resource
It grew for, should direct it? Every law
Of life, its every fitness, every flaw,
Must One determine whose corporeal shape
Would be no other than the prime escape
And revelation to me of a Will
Orb-like o'ershrouded and inscrutable
Above, save at the point which, I should know,
Shone that myself, my powers, might overflow
So far, so much; as now it signified
Which earthly shape it henceforth chose my guide,
Whose mortal lip selected to declare
Its oracles, what fleshly garb would wear
—The first of intimations, whom to love;
The next, how love him. Seemed that orb, above
The castle-covert and the mountain-close,
Slow in appearing,—if beneath it rose
Cravings, aversions,—did our green precinct
Take pride in me, at unawares distinct
With this or that endowment,—how, repressed
At once, such jetting power shrank to the rest!
Was I to have a chance touch spoil me, leave
My spirit thence unfitted to receive
The consummating spell?—that spell so near
Moreover! 'Waits he not the waking year?
His almond-blossoms must be honey-ripe
By this; to welcome him, fresh runnels stripe
The thawed ravines; because of him, the wind
Walks like a herald. I shall surely find
Him now!'

"And chief, that earnest April morn
Of Richard's Love-court, was it time, so worn
[Sidenote: A reverse to, and completion of, his.]
And white my cheek, so idly my blood beat,
Sitting that morn beside the Lady's feet
And saying as she prompted; till outburst
One face from all the faces. Not then first
I knew it; where in maple chamber glooms,

Crowned with what sanguine-heart pomegranate blooms
Advanced it ever? Men's acknowledgment
Sanctioned my own: 't was taken, Palma's bent,—
Sordello,—recognized, accepted.

"Dumb
Sat she still scheming. Ecelin would come
Gaunt, scared, 'Cesano baffles me,' he 'd say:
'Better I fought it out, my father's way!
Strangle Ferrara in its drowning flats,
And you and your Taurello yonder!—what 's
Romano's business there?' An hour's concern
To cure the froward Chief!—induce return
As heartened from those overmeaning eyes,
Wound up to persevere,—his enterprise
Marked out anew, its exigent of wit
Apportioned,—she at liberty to sit
And scheme against the next emergence, I—
To covet her Taurello-sprite, made fly
Or fold the wing—to con your horoscope
For leave command those steely shafts shoot ope,
Or straight assuage their blinding eagerness
In blank smooth snow. What semblance of success
To any of my plans for making you
[Sidenote: How she ever aspired for his sake,]
Mine and Romano's? Break the first wall through,
Tread o'er the ruins of the Chief, supplant
His sons beside, still, vainest were the vaunt:
There, Salinguerra would obstruct me sheer,
And the insuperable Tuscan, here,
Stay me! But one wild eve that Lady died
In her lone chamber: only I beside:
Taurello far at Naples, and my sire
At Padua, Ecelin away in ire
With Alberic. She held me thus—a clutch
[Sidenote: Circumstances helping or hindering.]
To make our spirits as our bodies touch—
And so began flinging the past up, heaps
Of uncouth treasure from their sunless sleeps
Within her soul; deeds rose along with dreams,
Fragments of many miserable schemes,
Secrets, more secrets, then—no, not the last—
'Mongst others, like a casual trick o' the past,
How ... ay, she told me, gathering up her face,
All left of it, into one arch-grimace
To die with ...

"Friend, 't is gone! but not the fear
Of that fell laughing, heard as now I hear.
Nor faltered voice, nor seemed her heart grow weak
When i' the midst abrupt she ceased to speak

—Dead, as to serve a purpose, mark!—for in
Rushed o' the very instant Ecelin
(How summoned, who divines?)—looking as if
He understood why Adelaide lay stiff
Already in my arms; for, 'Girl, how must
I manage Este in the matter thrust
Upon me, how unravel your bad coil?—
Since' (he declared) ''t is on your brow—a soil
Like hers there!' then in the same breath, 'he lacked
No counsel after all, had signed no pact
With devils, nor was treason here or there,
Goito or Vicenza, his affair:
He buried it in Adelaide's deep grave,
Would begin life afresh, now,—would not slave
For any Friedrich's nor Taurello's sake!
What booted him to meddle or to make
In Lombardy?' And afterward I knew
The meaning of his promise to undo
All she had done—why marriages were made,
New friendships entered on, old followers paid
With curses for their pains,—new friends' amaze
At height, when, passing out by Gate Saint Blaise,
He stopped short in Vicenza, bent his head
Over a friar's neck,—'had vowed,' he said,
'Long since, nigh thirty years, because his wife
And child were saved there, to bestow his life
On God, his gettings on the Church.'

"Exiled
Within Goito, still one dream beguiled
[Sidenote: How success at last seemed possible,]
My days and nights; 't was found, the orb I sought
To serve, those glimpses came of Fomalhaut,
No other: but how serve it?—authorize
You and Romano mingled destinies?
And straight Romano's angel stood beside
Me who had else been Boniface's bride,
For Salinguerra 't was, with neck low bent,
And voice lightened to music, (as he meant
To learn, not teach me,) who withdrew the pall
From the dead past and straight revived it all,
Making me see how first Romano waxed,
Wherefore he waned now, why, if I relaxed
My grasp (even I!) would drop a thing effete,
Frayed by itself, unequal to complete
Its course, and counting every step astray
[Sidenote: By the intervention of Salinguerra:]
A gain so much. Romano, every way
Stable, a Lombard House now—why start back
Into the very outset of its track?
This patching principle which late allied

Our House with other Houses—what beside
Concerned the apparition, the first Knight
Who followed Conrad hither in such plight
His utmost wealth was summed in his one steed?
For Ecelo, that prowler, was decreed
A task, in the beginning hazardous
To him as ever task can be to us;
But did the weather-beaten thief despair
When first our crystal cincture of warm air,
That binds the Trevisan,—as its spice-belt
(Crusaders say) the tract where Jesus dwelt,—
Furtive he pierced, and Este was to face—
Despaired Saponian strength of Lombard grace?
Tried he at making surer aught made sure,
Maturing what already was mature?
No; his heart prompted Ecelo, 'Confront
Este, inspect yourself. What 's nature? Wont.
Discard three-parts your nature, and adopt
[Sidenote: Who remedied ill wrought by Ecelin,]
The rest as an advantage!' Old strength propped
The man who first grew Podesta among
The Vicentines, no less than, while there sprung
His palace up in Padua like a threat,
Their noblest spied a grace, unnoticed yet
In Conrad's crew. Thus far the object gained,
Romano was established—has remained—
'For are you not Italian, truly peers
With Este? "Azzo" better soothes our ears
Than "Alberic"? or is this lion's-crine
From over-mounts' (this yellow hair of mine)
'So weak a graft on Agnes Este's stock?'
(Thus went he on with something of a mock)
'Wherefore recoil, then, from the very fate
Conceded you, refuse to imitate
Your model farther? Este long since left
Being mere Este: as a blade its heft,
Este required the Pope to further him;
And you, the Kaiser—whom your father's whim
Foregoes or, better, never shall forego
If Palma dare pursue what Ecelo
Commenced, but Ecelin desists from: just
As Adelaide of Susa could intrust
Her donative,—her Piedmont given the Pope,
Her Alpine-pass for him to shut or ope
'Twixt France and Italy,—to the superb
Matilda's perfecting,—so, lest aught curb
Our Adelaide's great counter-project for
Giving her Trentine to the Emperor
With passage here from Germany,—shall you
Take it,—my slender plodding talent, too!'
—Urged me Taurello with his half-smile.

"He
As Patron of the scattered family
Conveyed me to his Mantua, kept in bruit
Azzo's alliances and Richard's suit
Until, the Kaiser excommunicate,
'Nothing remains,' Taurello said, 'but wait
Some rash procedure: Palma was the link,
As Agnes' child, between us, and they shrink
[Sidenote: And had a project for her own glory,]
From losing Palma: judge if we advance,
Your father's method, your inheritance!'
The day I was betrothed to Boniface
At Padua by Taurello's self, took place
The outrage of the Ferrarese: again,
The day I sought Verona with the train
Agreed for,—by Taurello's policy
Convicting Richard of the fault, since we
Were present to annul or to confirm,—
Richard, whose patience had outstayed its term,
Quitted Verona for the siege.

"And now
What glory may engird Sordello's brow
Through this? A month since at Oliero slunk
All that was Ecelin into a monk;
But how could Salinguerra so forget
His liege of thirty years as grudge even yet
One effort to recover him? He sent
Forthwith the tidings of this last event
To Ecelin—declared that he, despite
The recent folly, recognized his right
To order Salinguerra: 'Should he wring
Its uttermost advantage out, or fling
This chance away? Or were his sons now Head
O' the House?' Through me Taurello's missive sped;
My father's answer will by me return.
Behold! 'For him,' he writes, 'no more concern
With strife than, for his children, with fresh plots
Of Friedrich. Old engagements out he blots
For aye: Taurello shall no more subserve,
Nor Ecelin impose.' Lest this unnerve
Taurello at this juncture, slack his grip
Of Richard, suffer the occasion slip,—
I, in his sons' default (who, mating with
Este, forsake Romano as the frith
Its mainsea for that firmland, sea makes head
Against) I stand, Romano,—in their stead
Assume the station they desert, and give
Still, as the Kaiser's representative,
Taurello license he demands. Midnight—

Morning—by noon to-morrow, making light
[Sidenote: Which she would change to Sordello's.]
Of the League's issue, we, in some gay weed
Like yours, disguised together, may precede
The arbitrators to Ferrara: reach
Him, let Taurello's noble accents teach
The rest! Then say if I have misconceived
Your destiny, too readily believed
The Kaiser's cause your own!"

And Palma 's fled.
Though no affirmative disturbs the head,
A dying lamp-flame sinks and rises o'er,
Like the alighted planet Pollux wore,
Until, morn breaking, he resolves to be
Gate-vein of this heart's blood of Lombardy,
Soul of this body—to wield this aggregate
Of souls and bodies, and so conquer fate
Though he should live—a centre of disgust
Even—apart, core of the outward crust
He vivifies, assimilates. For thus
I bring Sordello to the rapturous
[Sidenote: Thus then, having completed a circle,]
Exclaim at the crowd's cry, because one round
Of life was quite accomplished; and he found
Not only that a soul, whate'er its might,
Is insufficient to its own delight,
Both in corporeal organs and in skill
By means of such to body forth its Will—
And, after, insufficient to apprise
Men of that Will, oblige them recognize
The Hid by the Revealed—but that, the last
Nor lightest of the struggles overpast,
Will he bade abdicate, which would not void
The throne, might sit there, suffer he enjoyed
Mankind, a varied and divine array
Incapable of homage, the first way,
Nor fit to render incidentally
Tribute connived at, taken by the by,
In joys. If thus with warrant to rescind
The ignominious exile of mankind—
Whose proper service, ascertained intact
As yet, (to be by him themselves made act,
Not watch Sordello acting each of them)
Was to secure—if the true diadem
Seemed imminent while our Sordello drank
The wisdom of that golden Palma,—thank
Verona's Lady in her citadel
Founded by Gaulish Brennus, legends tell:
And truly when she left him, the sun reared
A head like the first clamberer's who peered

A-top the Capitol, his face on flame
With triumph, triumphing till Manlius came.
Nor slight too much my rhymes—that spring, dispread,
Dispart, disperse, lingering overhead
Like an escape of angels! Rather say,
[Sidenote: The poet may pause and breathe,]
My transcendental platan! mounting gay
(An archimage so courts a novice-queen)
With tremulous silvered trunk, whence branches sheen
Laugh out, thick foliaged next, a-shiver soon
With colored buds, then glowing like the moon
One mild flame,—last a pause, a burst, and all
Her ivory limbs are smothered by a fall,
Bloom-flinders and fruit-sparkles and leaf-dust,
Ending the weird work prosecuted just
For her amusement; he decrepit, stark,
Dozes; her uncontrolled delight may mark
Apart—

Yet not so, surely never so!
Only, as good my soul were suffered go
O'er the lagune: forth fare thee, put aside—
Entrance thy synod, as a god may glide
Out of the world he fills, and leave it mute
For myriad ages as we men compute,
Returning into it without a break
[Sidenote: Being really in the flesh at Venice.]
O' the consciousness! They sleep, and I awake
O'er the lagune, being at Venice.

Note,
In just such songs as Eglamor (say) wrote
With heart and soul and strength, for he believed
Himself achieving all to be achieved
By singer—in such songs you find alone
Completeness, judge the song and singer one,
And either purpose answered, his in it
Or its in him: while from true works (to wit
Sordello's dream-performances that will
Never be more than dreamed) escapes there still
Some proof, the singer's proper life was 'neath
The life his song exhibits, this a sheath
To that; a passion and a knowledge far
Transcending these, majestic as they are,
Smouldered; his lay was but an episode
In the bard's life: which evidence you owed
To some slight weariness, some looking-off
Or start-away. The childish skit or scoff
In "Charlemagne," (his poem, dreamed divine
In every point except one silly line
About the restiff daughters)—what may lurk

In that? "My life commenced before this work,"
(So I interpret the significance
Of the bard's start aside and look askance)—
"My life continues after: on I fare
With no more stopping, possibly, no care
[Sidenote: And watching his own life sometimes,]
To note the undercurrent, the why and how,
Where, when, o' the deeper life, as thus just now.
But, silent, shall I cease to live? Alas
For you! who sigh, 'When shall it come to pass
We read that story? How will he compress
The future gains, his life's true business,
Into the better lay which—that one flout,
Howe'er inopportune it be, lets out—
Engrosses him already, though professed
To meditate with us eternal rest,
And partnership in all his life has found?'"
'T is but a sailor's promise, weather-bound:
"Strike sail, slip cable, here the bark be moored
For once, the awning stretched, the poles assured!
Noontide above; except the wave's crisp dash,
Or buzz of colibri, or tortoise' splash,
The margin 's silent: out with every spoil
Made in our tracking, coil by mighty coil,
This serpent of a river to his head
I' the midst! Admire each treasure, as we spread
The bank, to help us tell our history
Aright: give ear, endeavor to descry
The groves of giant rushes, how they grew
Like demons' endlong tresses we sailed through,
What mountains yawned, forests to give us vent
Opened, each doleful side, yet on we went
Till ... may that beetle (shake your cap) attest
The springing of a land-wind from the West!"
—Wherefore? Ah yes, you frolic it to-day!
To-morrow, and, the pageant moved away
Down to the poorest tent-pole, we and you
Part company: no other may pursue
Eastward your voyage, be informed what fate
Intends, if triumph or decline await
The tempter of the everlasting steppe.
I muse this on a ruined palace-step
At Venice: why should I break off, nor sit
Longer upon my step, exhaust the fit
England gave birth to? Who 's adorable
Enough reclaim a—no Sordello's Will
Alack!—be queen to me? That Bassanese
Busied among her smoking fruit-boats? These
Perhaps from our delicious Asolo
Who twinkle, pigeons o'er the portico
Not prettier, bind June lilies into sheaves

To deck the bridge-side chapel, dropping leaves
[Sidenote: Because it is pleasant to be young,]
Soiled by their own loose gold-meal?
Ah, beneath
The cool arch stoops she, brownest cheek! Her wreath
Endures a month—a half month—if I make
A queen of her, continue for her sake
Sordello's story? Nay, that Paduan girl
Splashes with barer legs where a live whirl
In the dead black Giudecca proves sea-weed
Drifting has sucked down three, four, all indeed
Save one pale-red striped, pale-blue turbaned post
For gondolas.

You sad dishevelled ghost
That pluck at me and point, are you advised
I breathe? Let stay those girls (e'en her disguised
—Jewels i' the locks that love no crownet like
Their native field-buds and the green wheat-spike,
So fair!—who left this end of June's turmoil,
Shook off, as might a lily its gold soil,
Pomp, save a foolish gem or two, and free
In dream, came join the peasants o'er the sea).
Look they too happy, too tricked out? Confess
There is such niggard stock of happiness
To share, that, do one's uttermost, dear wretch,
One labors ineffectually to stretch
[Sidenote: Would but suffering humanity allow!]
It o'er you so that mother and children, both
May equitably flaunt the sumpter-cloth!
Divide the robe yet farther: be content
With seeing just a score pre-eminent
Through shreds of it, acknowledged happy wights,
Engrossing what should furnish all, by rights!
For, these in evidence, you clearlier claim
A like garb for the rest,—grace all, the same
As these my peasants. I ask youth and strength
And health for each of you, not more—at length
Grown wise, who asked at home that the whole race
Might add the spirit's to the body's grace,
And all be dizened out as chiefs and bards.
But in this magic weather one discards
Much old requirement. Venice seems a type
Of Life—'twixt blue and blue extends, a stripe,
As Life, the somewhat, hangs 'twixt naught and naught:
'T is Venice, and 't is Life—as good you sought
To spare me the Piazza's slippery stone
Or keep me to the unchoked canals alone,
As hinder Life the evil with the good
Which make up Living, rightly understood.
[Sidenote: Which instigates to tasks like this,]

Only, do finish something! Peasants, queens,
Take them, made happy by whatever means,
Parade them for the common credit, vouch
That a luckless residue, we send to crouch
In corners out of sight, was just as framed
For happiness, its portion might have claimed
As well, and so, obtaining joy, had stalked
Fastuous as any!—such my project, balked
Already; I hardly venture to adjust
The first rags, when you find me. To mistrust
Me!—nor unreasonably. You, no doubt,
Have the true knack of tiring suitors out
With those thin lips on tremble, lashless eyes
Inveterately tear-shot—there, be wise,
Mistress of mine, there, there, as if I meant
You insult!—shall your friend (not slave) be shent
For speaking home? Beside, care-bit erased
Broken-up beauties ever took my taste
Supremely; and I love you more, far more
Than her I looked should foot Life's temple-floor.
Years ago, leagues at distance, when and where
A whisper came, "Let others seek!—thy care
[Sidenote: And doubtlessly compensates them,]
Is found, thy life's provision; if thy race
Should be thy mistress, and into one face
The many faces crowd?" Ah, had I, judge,
Or no, your secret? Rough apparel—grudge
All ornaments save tag or tassel worn
To hint we are not thoroughly forlorn—
Slouch bonnet, unloop mantle, careless go
Alone (that 's saddest, but it must be so)
Through Venice, sing now and now glance aside,
Aught desultory or undignified,—
Then, ravishingest lady, will you pass
Or not each formidable group, the mass
Before the Basilic (that feast gone by,
God's great day of the Corpus Domini)
And, wistfully foregoing proper men,
Come timid up to me for alms? And then
The luxury to hesitate, feign do
Some unexampled grace!—when, whom but you
Dare I bestow your own upon? And hear
Further before you say, it is to sneer
I call you ravishing; for I regret
Little that she, whose early foot was set
Forth as she 'd plant it on a pedestal,
Now, i' the silent city, seems to fall
Toward me—no wreath, only a lip's unrest
To quiet, surcharged eyelids to be pressed
Dry of their tears upon my bosom. Strange
Such sad chance should produce in thee such change,

My love! Warped souls and bodies! yet God spoke
Of right-hand, foot and eye—selects our yoke,
Sordello, as your poetship may find!
So, sleep upon my shoulder, child, nor mind
Their foolish talk; we 'll manage reinstate
Your old worth; ask moreover, when they prate
Of evil men past hope, "Don't each contrive,
Despite the evil you abuse, to live?—
Keeping, each losel, through a maze of lies,
His own conceit of truth? to which he hies
By obscure windings, tortuous, if you will,
But to himself not inaccessible;
He sees truth, and his lies are for the crowd
Who cannot see; some fancied right allowed
His vilest wrong, empowered the losel clutch
One pleasure from a multitude of such
[Sidenote: As those who desist should remember.]
Denied him." Then assert, "All men appear
To think all better than themselves, by here
Trusting a crowd they wrong; but really," say,
"All men think all men stupider than they,
Since, save themselves, no other comprehends
The complicated scheme to make amends
—Evil, the scheme by which, through Ignorance,
Good labors to exist." A slight advance,—
Merely to find the sickness you die through,
And naught beside! but if one can't eschew
One's portion in the common lot, at least
One can avoid an ignorance increased
Tenfold by dealing out hint after hint
How naught were like dispensing without stint
The water of life—so easy to dispense
Beside, when one has probed the centre whence
Commotion 's born—could tell you of it all!
"—Meantime, just meditate my madrigal
O' the mugwort that conceals a dewdrop safe!"
What, dullard? we and you in smothery chafe,
Babes, baldheads, stumbled thus far into Zin
The Horrid, getting neither out nor in,
A hungry sun above us, sands that bung
Our throats,—each dromedary lolls a tongue,
Each camel churns a sick and frothy chap,
And you, 'twixt tales of Potiphar's mishap,
And sonnets on the earliest ass that spoke,
—Remark, you wonder any one needs choke
With founts about! Potsherd him, Gibeonites!
While awkwardly enough your Moses smites
The rock, though he forego his Promised Land
Thereby, have Satan claim his carcass, and
Figure as Metaphysic Poet ... ah,
Mark ye the dim first oozings? Meribah!

Then, quaffing at the fount my courage gained,
Recall—not that I prompt ye—who explained ...
"Presumptuous!" interrupts one. You, not I
'T is, brother, marvel at and magnify
[Sidenote: Let the poet take his own part, then,]
Such office: "office," quotha? can we get
To the beginning of the office yet?
What do we here? simply experiment
Each on the other's power and its intent
When elsewhere tasked,—if this of mine were trucked
For yours to either's good,—we watch construct,
In short, an engine: with a finished one,
What it can do, is all,—naught, how 't is done.
But this of ours yet in probation, dusk
A kernel of strange wheelwork through its husk
Grows into shape by quarters and by halves;
Remark this tooth's spring, wonder what that valve's
Fall bodes, presume each faculty's device,
Make out each other more or less precise—
The scope of the whole engine 's to be proved;
We die: which means to say, the whole 's removed,
Dismounted wheel by wheel, this complex gin,—
To be set up anew elsewhere, begin
A task indeed, but with a clearer clime
Than the murk lodgment of our building-time.
And then, I grant you, it behoves forget
How 't is done—all that must amuse us yet
So long: and, while you turn upon your heel,
Pray that I be not busy slitting steel
[Sidenote: Should any object that he was dull]
Or shredding brass, camped on some virgin shore
Under a cluster of fresh stars, before
I name a tithe o' the wheels I trust to do!
So occupied, then, are we: hitherto,
At present, and a weary while to come,
The office of ourselves,—nor blind nor dumb,
And seeing somewhat of man's state,—has been,
For the worst of us, to say they so have seen;
For the better, what it was they saw; the best
Impart the gift of seeing to the rest:
"So that I glance," says such an one, "around,
And there 's no face but I can read profound
Disclosures in; this stands for hope, that—fear,
And for a speech, a deed in proof, look here!
'Stoop, else the strings of blossom, where the nuts
O'erarch, will blind thee! Said I not? She shuts
Both eyes this time, so close the hazels meet!
Thus, prisoned in the Piombi, I repeat
Events one rove occasioned, o'er and o'er,
Putting 'twixt me and madness evermore
Thy sweet shape, Zanze! Therefore stoop!'

'That's truth!'
(Adjudge you) 'the incarcerated youth
Would say that!'

Youth? Plara the bard? Set down
That Plara spent his youth in a grim town
Whose cramped ill-featured streets huddled about
The minster for protection, never out
Of its black belfry's shade and its bells' roar.
The brighter shone the suburb,—all the more
Ugly and absolute that shade's reproof
Of any chance escape of joy,—some roof,
Taller than they, allowed the rest detect,—
Before the sole permitted laugh (suspect
Who could, 't was meant for laughter, that ploughed cheek's
Repulsive gleam!) when the sun stopped both peaks
Of the cleft belfry like a fiery wedge,
Then sank, a huge flame on its socket edge,
With leavings on the gray glass oriel-pane
Ghastly some minutes more. No fear of rain—
The minster minded that! in heaps the dust
Lay everywhere. This town, the minster's trust,
[Sidenote: Beside his sprightlier predecessors.]
Held Plara; who, its denizen, bade hail
In twice twelve sonnets, Tempe's dewy vale."
"'Exact the town, the minster and the street!'"
"As all mirth triumphs, sadness means defeat:
Lust triumphs and is gay, Love 's triumphed o'er
And sad: but Lucio 's sad. I said before,
Love 's sad, not Lucio; one who loves may be
As gay his love has leave to hope, as he
Downcast that lusts' desire escapes the springe:
'T is of the mood itself I speak, what tinge
Determines it, else colorless,—or mirth,
Or melancholy, as from heaven or earth."
"'Ay, that's the variation's gist!'

Indeed?
Thus far advanced in safety then, proceed!
And having seen too what I saw, be bold
And next encounter what I do behold
(That 's sure) but bid you take on trust!"

Attack
The use and purpose of such sights? Alack,
Not so unwisely does the crowd dispense
On Salinguerras praise in preference
[Sidenote: One ought not blame but praise this;]
To the Sordellos: men of action, these!
Who, seeing just as little as you please,

Yet turn that little to account,—engage
With, do not gaze at,—carry on, a stage,
The work o' the world, not merely make report
The work existed ere their day! In short,
When at some future no-time a brave band
Sees, using what it sees, then shake my hand
In heaven, my brother! Meanwhile where 's the hurt
Of keeping the Makers-see on the alert,
At whose defection mortals stare aghast
As though heaven's bounteous windows were slammed fast
Incontinent? Whereas all you, beneath,
Should scowl at, bruise their lips and break their teeth
Who ply the pullies, for neglecting you:
And therefore have I moulded, made anew
A Man, and give him to be turned and tried,
Be angry with or pleased at. On your side,
Have ye times, places, actors of your own?
[Sidenote: At all events, his own audience may:]
Try them upon Sordello when full-grown,
And then—ah then! If Hercules first parched
His foot in Egypt only to be marched
A sacrifice for Jove with pomp to suit,
What chance have I? The demigod was mute
Till, at the altar, where time out of mind
Such guests became oblations, chaplets twined
His forehead long enough, and he began
Slaying the slayers, nor escaped a man.
Take not affront, my gentle audience! whom
No Hercules shall make his hecatomb,
Believe, nor from his brows your chaplet rend—
That's your kind suffrage, yours, my patron-friend,
Whose great verse blares unintermittent on
Like your own trumpeter at Marathon,—
You who, Platæa and Salamis being scant,
Put up with Ætna for a stimulant—
And did well, I acknowledged, as he loomed
Over the midland sea last month, presumed
Long, lay demolished in the blazing West
At eve, while towards him tilting cloudlets pressed
Like Persian ships at Salamis. Friend, wear
A crest proud as desert while I declare
Had I a flawless ruby fit to wring
Tears of its color from that painted king
Who lost it, I would, for that smile which went
To my heart, fling it in the sea, content,
[Sidenote: What if things brighten, who knows?]
Wearing your verse in place, an amulet
Sovereign against all passion, wear and fret!
My English Eyebright, if you are not glad
That, as I stopped my task awhile, the sad
Dishevelled form, wherein I put mankind

To come at times and keep my pact in mind,
Renewed me,—hear no crickets in the hedge,
Nor let a glowworm spot the river's edge
At home, and may the summer showers gush
Without a warning from the missel thrush!
So, to our business, now—the fate of such
As find our common nature—overmuch
Despised because restricted and unfit
To bear the burden they impose on it—
Cling when they would discard it; craving strength
To leap from the allotted world, at length
They do leap,—flounder on without a term,
Each a god's germ, doomed to remain a germ
In unexpanded infancy, unless ...
But that 's the story—dull enough, confess!
There might be fitter subjects to allure;
Still, neither misconceive my portraiture
Nor undervalue its adornments quaint:
What seems a fiend perchance may prove a saint.
Ponder a story ancient pens transmit,
Then say if you condemn me or acquit.

John the Beloved, banished Antioch
For Patmos, bade collectively his flock
[Sidenote: Whereupon, with a story to the point,]
Farewell, but set apart the closing eve
To comfort those his exile most would grieve,
He knew: a touching spectacle, that house
In motion to receive him! Xanthus' spouse
You missed, made panther's meat a month since; but
Xanthus himself (his nephew 't was, they shut
'Twixt boards and sawed asunder), Polycarp,
Soft Charicle, next year no wheel could warp
To swear by Cæsar's fortune, with the rest
Were ranged; through whom the gray disciple pressed,
Busily blessing right and left, just stopped
To pat one infant's curls, the hangman cropped
Soon after, reached the portal. On its hinge
The door turns and he enters: what quick twinge
Ruins the smiling mouth, those wide eyes fix
Whereon, why like some spectral candlestick's
Branch the disciple's arms? Dead swooned he, woke
Anon, heaved sigh, made shift to gasp, heartbroke,
"Get thee behind me, Satan! Have I toiled
To no more purpose? Is the gospel foiled
Here too, and o'er my son's, my Xanthus' hearth,
Portrayed with sooty garb and features swarth—
Ah, Xanthus, am I to thy roof beguiled
To see the—the—the Devil domiciled?"
Whereto sobbed Xanthus, "Father, 't is yourself
Installed, a limning which our utmost pelf

Went to procure against to-morrow's loss;
[Sidenote: *He takes up the thread of discourse.*]
And that's no twy-prong, but a pastoral cross,
You're painted with!"

His puckered brows unfold—
And you shall hear Sordello's story told.

BOOK THE FOURTH

Meantime Ferrara lay in rueful case;
The lady-city, for whose sole embrace
Her pair of suitors struggled, felt their arms
A brawny mischief to the fragile charms
They tugged for—one discovering that to twist
Her tresses twice or thrice about his wrist
Secured a point of vantage—one, how best
He 'd parry that by planting in her breast
His elbow spike—each party too intent
[Sidenote: *Men suffered much,*]
For noticing, howe'er the battle went,
The conqueror would but have a corpse to kiss.
"May Boniface be duly damned for this!"
—Howled some old Ghibellin, as up he turned,
From the wet heap of rubbish where they burned
His house, a little skull with dazzling teeth:
"A boon, sweet Christ—let Salinguerra seethe
In hell forever, Christ, and let myself
Be there to laugh at him!"—moaned some young Guelf
Stumbling upon a shrivelled hand nailed fast
To the charred lintel of the doorway, last
His father stood within to bid him speed.
The thoroughfares were overrun with weed
—Docks, quitchgrass, loathy mallows no man plants.
The stranger, none of its inhabitants
[Sidenote: *Whichever of the parties was victor.*]
Crept out of doors to taste fresh air again,
And ask the purpose of a splendid train
Admitted on a morning; every town
Of the East League was come by envoy down
To treat for Richard's ransom: here you saw
The Vicentine, here snowy oxen draw
The Paduan carroch, its vermilion cross
On its white field. A-tiptoe o'er the fosse
Looked Legate Montelungo wistfully
After the flock of steeples he might spy
In Este's time, gone (doubts he) long ago
To mend the ramparts: sure the laggards know
The Pope 's as good as here! They paced the streets

More soberly. At last, "Taurello greets
The League," announced a pursuivant,—"will match
Its courtesy, and labors to dispatch
At earliest Tito, Friedrich's Pretor, sent
On pressing matters from his post at Trent,
With Mainard Count of Tyrol,—simply waits
Their going to receive the delegates."
"Tito!" Our delegates exchanged a glance,
And, keeping the main way, admired askance
The lazy engines of outlandish birth,
Couched like a king each on its bank of earth—
Arbalist, manganel and catapult;
While stationed by, as waiting a result,
Lean silent gangs of mercenaries ceased
Working to watch the strangers. "This, at least,
Were better spared; he scarce presumes gainsay
The League's decision! Get our friend away
And profit for the future: how else teach
Fools 't is not safe to stray within claw's reach
Ere Salinguerra's final gasp be blown?
Those mere convulsive scratches find the bone.
Who bade him bloody the spent osprey's nare?"
The carrochs halted in the public square.
Pennons of every blazon once a-flaunt,
Men prattled, freelier that the crested gaunt
[Sidenote: How Guelfs criticise Ghibellin work]
White ostrich with a horse-shoe in her beak
Was missing, and whoever chose might speak
"Ecelin" boldly out: so,—"Ecelin
Needed his wife to swallow half the sin
And sickens by himself: the devil's whelp,
He styles his son, dwindles away, no help
From conserves, your fine triple-curded froth
Of virgin's blood, your Venice viper-broth—
Eh? Jubilate!"—"Peace! no little word
You utter here that 's not distinctly heard
Up at Oliero: he was absent sick
When we besieged Bassano—who, i' the thick
O' the work, perceived the progress Azzo made,
Like Ecelin, through his witch Adelaide?
She managed it so well that, night by night,
At their bed-foot stood up a soldier-sprite,
First fresh, pale by-and-by without a wound,
And, when it came with eyes filmed as in swound,
They knew the place was taken."—"Ominous
That Ghibellins should get what cautelous
Old Redbeard sought from Azzo's sire to wrench
Vainly; Saint George contrived his town a trench
O' the marshes, an impermeable bar."
"—Young Ecelin is meant the tutelar
Of Padua, rather; veins embrace upon

His hand like Brenta and Bacchiglion."
What now?—"The founts! God's bread, touch not a plank!
A crawling hell of carrion—every tank
[Sidenote: As unusually energetic in this case.]
Choke full!—found out just now to Cino's cost—
The same who gave Taurello up for lost,
And, making no account of fortune's freaks,
Refused to budge from Padua then, but sneaks
Back now with Concorezzi—'faith! they drag
Their carroch to San Vitale, plant the flag
On his own palace, so adroitly razed
He knew it not; a sort of Guelf folk gazed
And laughed apart; Cino disliked their air—
Must pluck up spirit, show he does not care—
Seats himself on the tank's edge—will begin
To hum, za, za, Cavaler Ecelin—
A silence; he gets warmer, clinks to chime,
Now both feet plough the ground, deeper each time,
At last, za, za, and up with a fierce kick
Comes his own mother's face caught by the thick
Gray hair about his spur!"

Which means, they lift
The covering, Salinguerra made a shift
To stretch upon the truth; as well avoid
Further disclosures; leave them thus employed.
Our dropping Autumn morning clears apace,
And poor Ferrara puts a softened face
On her misfortunes. Let us scale this tall
Huge foursquare line of red brick garden-wall
[Sidenote: How, passing through the rare garden,]
Bastioned within by trees of every sort
On three sides, slender, spreading, long and short;
Each grew as it contrived, the poplar ramped,
The fig-tree reared itself,—but stark and cramped,
Made fools of, like tamed lions: whence, on the edge,
Running 'twixt trunk and trunk to smooth one ledge
Of shade, were shrubs inserted, warp and woof,
Which smothered up that variance. Scale the roof
Of solid tops, and o'er the slope you slide
Down to a grassy space level and wide,
Here and there dotted with a tree, but trees
Of rarer leaf, each foreigner at ease,
Set by itself: and in the centre spreads,
Borne upon three uneasy leopards' heads,
A laver, broad and shallow, one bright spirt
Of water bubbles in. The walls begirt
With trees leave off on either hand; pursue
Your path along a wondrous avenue
Those walls abut on, heaped of gleamy stone,
With aloes leering everywhere, gray-grown

From many a Moorish summer: how they wind
Out of the fissures! likelier to bind
The building than those rusted cramps which drop
Already in the eating sunshine. Stop,
You fleeting shapes above there! Ah, the pride
Or else despair of the whole country-side!
A range of statues, swarming o'er with wasps,
[Sidenote: Salinguerra contrived for a purpose,]
God, goddess, woman, man, the Greek rough-rasps
In crumbling Naples marble—meant to look
Like those Messina marbles Constance took
Delight in, or Taurello's self conveyed
To Mantua for his mistress, Adelaide,
A certain font with caryatides
Since cloistered at Goito; only, these
Are up and doing, not abashed, a troop
Able to right themselves—who see you, stoop
Their arms o' the instant after you! Unplucked
By this or that, you pass; for they conduct
To terrace raised on terrace, and, between,
Creatures of brighter mould and braver mien
Than any yet, the choicest of the Isle
No doubt. Here, left a sullen breathing-while,
Up-gathered on himself the Fighter stood
For his last fight, and, wiping treacherous blood
Out of the eyelids just held ope beneath
Those shading fingers in their iron sheath,
Steadied his strengths amid the buzz and stir
Of the dusk hideous amphitheatre
At the announcement of his over-match
To wind the day's diversion up, dispatch
The pertinacious Gaul: while, limbs one heap,
The Slave, no breath in her round mouth, watched leap
Dart after dart forth, as her hero's car
Clove dizzily the solid of the war
—Let coil about his knees for pride in him.
We reach the farthest terrace, and the grim
San Pietro Palace stops us.

Such the state
Of Salinguerra's plan to emulate
Sicilian marvels, that his girlish wife
Retrude still might lead her ancient life
In her new home: whereat enlarged so much
Neighbors upon the novel princely touch
He took,—who here imprisons Boniface.
Here must the Envoys come to sue for grace;
And here, emerging from the labyrinth
Below, Sordello paused beside the plinth
Of the door-pillar.
[Sidenote: Sordello ponders all seen and heard,]

He had really left
Verona for the cornfields (a poor theft
From the morass) where Este's camp was made.
The Envoys' march, the Legate's cavalcade—
All had been seen by him, but scarce as when,—
Eager for cause to stand aloof from men
At every point save the fantastic tie
Acknowledged in his boyish sophistry,—
He made account of such. A crowd,—he meant
To task the whole of it; each part's intent
Concerned him therefore: and, the more he pried,
The less became Sordello satisfied
With his own figure at the moment. Sought
He respite from his task? Descried he aught
Novel in the anticipated sight
Of all these livers upon all delight?
This phalanx, as of myriad points combined,
Whereby he still had imaged the mankind
His youth was passed in dreams of rivalling,
His age—in plans to prove at least such thing
Had been so dreamed,—which now he must impress
With his own will, effect a happiness
By theirs,—supply a body to his soul
Thence, and become eventually whole
With them as he had hoped to be without—
[Sidenote: Finds in men no machine for his sake,]
Made these the mankind he once raved about?
Because a few of them were notable,
Should all be figured worthy note? As well
Expect to find Taurello's triple line
Of trees a single and prodigious pine.
Real pines rose here and there; but, close among,
Thrust into and mixed up with pines, a throng
Of shrubs, he saw,—a nameless common sort
O'erpast in dreams, left out of the report
And hurried into corners, or at best
Admitted to be fancied like the rest.
Reckon that morning's proper chiefs—how few!
And yet the people grew, the people grew,
Grew ever, as if the many there indeed,
More left behind and most who should succeed,—
Simply in virtue of their mouths and eyes,
Petty enjoyments and huge miseries,—
Mingled with, and made veritably great
Those chiefs: he overlooked not Mainard's state
Nor Concorezzi's station, but instead
Of stopping there, each dwindled to be head
Of infinite and absent Tyrolese
Or Paduans; startling all the more, that these
Seemed passive and disposed of, uncared for,

Yet doubtless on the whole (like Eglamor)
Smiling; for if a wealthy man decays
And out of store of robes must wear, all days,
One tattered suit, alike in sun and shade,
'Tis commonly some tarnished gay brocade
Fit for a feast-night's flourish and no more:
Nor otherwise from poor Misery from her store
Of looks is fain upgather, keep unfurled
For common wear as she goes through the world,
The faint remainder of some worn-out smile
Meant for a feast-night's service merely. While
Crowd upon crowd rose on Sordello thus,—
(Crowds no way interfering to discuss,
Much less dispute, life's joys with one employed
In envying them,—or, if they aught enjoyed,
Where lingered something indefinable
In every look and tone, the mirth as well
As woe, that fixed at once his estimate
Of the result, their good or bad estate)—
[Sidenote: But a thing with life of its own,]
Old memories returned with new effect:
And the new body, ere he could suspect,
Cohered, mankind and he were really fused,
The new self seemed impatient to be used
By him, but utterly another way
Than that anticipated: strange to say,
They were too much below him, more in thrall
Than he, the adjunct than the principal.
What booted scattered units?—here a mind
And there, which might repay his own to find,
And stamp, and use?—a few, howe'er august,
If all the rest were grovelling in the dust?
No: first a mighty equilibrium, sure,
Should he establish, privilege procure
For all, the few had long possessed! He felt
An error, an exceeding error melt—
While he was occupied with Mantuan chants,
Behoved him think of men, and take their wants,
Such as he now distinguished every side,
As his own want which might be satisfied,—
And, after that, think of rare qualities
Of his own soul demanding exercise.
It followed naturally, through no claim
On their part, which made virtue of the aim
At serving them, on his,—that, past retrieve,
He felt now in their toils, theirs,—nor could leave
Wonder how, in the eagerness to rule,
Impress his will on mankind, he (the fool!)
Had never even entertained the thought
That this his last arrangement might be fraught
With incidental good to them as well,

[Sidenote: And rights hitherto ignored by him,]
And that mankind's delight would help to swell
His own. So, if he sighed, as formerly
Because the merry time of life must fleet,
'T was deeplier now,—for could the crowds repeat
Their poor experiences? His hand that shook
Was twice to be deplored. "The Legate, look!
With eyes, like fresh-blown thrush-eggs on a thread,
Faint-blue and loosely floating in his head,
Large tongue, moist open mouth; and this long while
That owner of the idiotic smile
[Sidenote: A fault he is now anxious to repair,]
Serves them!"

He fortunately saw in time
His fault however, and since the office prime
Includes the secondary—best accept
Both offices; Taurello, its adept,
Could teach him the preparatory one,
And how to do what he had fancied done
Long previously, ere take the greater task,
How render first these people happy? Ask
The people's friends: for there must be one good,
One way to it—the Cause!—he understood
The meaning now of Palma; why the jar
Else, the ado, the trouble wide and far
Of Guelfs and Ghibellins, the Lombard hope
And Rome's despair?—'twixt Emperor and Pope
The confused shifting sort of Eden tale—
Hardihood still recurring, still to fail—
That foreign interloping fiend, this free
And native overbrooding deity—
Yet a dire fascination o'er the palms
The Kaiser ruined, troubling even the calms
Of paradise—or, on the other hand,
[Sidenote: Since he apprehends its full extent,]
The Pontiff, as the Kaisers understand,
One snake-like cursed of God to love the ground,
Whose heavy length breaks in the noon profound
Some saving tree—which needs the Kaiser, dressed
As the dislodging angel of that pest,
Yet flames that pest bedropped, flat head, full fold,
With coruscating dower of dyes. "Behold
The secret, so to speak, and master-spring
O' the contest!—which of the two Powers shall bring
Men good—perchance the most good—ay, it may
Be that!—the question, which best knows the way."
And hereupon Count Mainard strutted past
Out of San Pietro; never seemed the last
Of archers, slingers: and our friend began
To recollect strange modes of serving man,

Arbalist, catapult, brake, manganel,
And more. "This way of theirs may,—who can tell?—
Need perfecting," said he: "let all be solved
At once! Taurello 't is, the task devolved
On late—confront Taurello!"

And at last
He did confront him. Scarce an hour had past
When forth Sordello came, older by years
Than at his entry. Unexampled fears
Oppressed him, and he staggered off, blind, mute
And deaf, like some fresh-mutilated brute,
Into Ferrara—not the empty town
That morning witnessed: he went up and down
Streets whence the veil had been stripped shred by shred,
So that, in place of huddling with their dead
Indoors, to answer Salinguerra's ends,
Townsfolk make shift to crawl forth, sit like friends
With any one. A woman gave him choice
Of her two daughters, the infantile voice
Or the dimpled knee, for half a chain, his throat
Was clasped with; but an archer knew the coat—
Its blue cross and eight lilies,—bade beware
One dogging him in concert with the pair
Though thrumming on the sleeve that hid his knife.
Night set in early, autumn dews were rife,
They kindled great fires while the Leaguers' mass
Began at every carroch—he must pass
Between the kneeling people. Presently
The carroch of Verona caught his eye
With purple trappings; silently he bent
Over its fire, when voices violent
Began, "Affirm not whom the youth was like
That struck me from the porch, I did not strike
Again: I too have chestnut hair; my kin
[Sidenote: And would fain have helped some way,]
Hate Azzo and stand up for Ecelin.
Here, minstrel, drive bad thoughts away! Sing! Take
My glove for guerdon!" And for that man's sake
He turned: "A song of Eglamor's!"—scarce named,
When, "Our Sordello's rather!"—all exclaimed;
"Is not Sordello famousest for rhyme?"
He had been happy to deny, this time,—
Profess as heretofore the aching head
And failing heart,—suspect that in his stead
Some true Apollo had the charge of them,
Was champion to reward or to condemn,
So his intolerable risk might shift
Or share itself; but Naddo's precious gift
Of gifts, he owned, be certain! At the close—
"I made that," said he to a youth who rose

As if to hear: 't was Palma through the band
Conducted him in silence by her hand.
Back now for Salinguerra. Tito of Trent
Gave place to Palma and her friend; who went
In turn at Montelungo's visit—one
After the other were they come and gone,—
These spokesmen for the Kaiser and the Pope,
This incarnation of the People's hope,
Sordello,—all the say of each was said;
And Salinguerra sat, himself instead
Of these to talk with, lingered musing yet.
'T was a drear vast presence-chamber roughly set
In order for the morning's use; full face,
The Kaiser's ominous sign-mark had first place,
The crowned grim twy-necked eagle, coarsely-blacked
With ochre on the naked wall; nor lacked
Romano's green and yellow either side;
But the new token Tito brought had tried
The Legate's patience—nay, if Palma knew
What Salinguerra almost meant to do
Until the sight of her restored his lip
A certain half-smile, three months' chieftainship
Had banished! Afterward, the Legate found
No change in him, nor asked what badge he wound
And unwound carelessly. Now sat the Chief
[Sidenote: But Salinguerra is also preoccupied;]
Silent as when our couple left, whose brief
Encounter wrought so opportune effect
In thoughts he summoned not, nor would reject,
Though time 't was now if ever, to pause—fix
On any sort of ending; wiles and tricks
Exhausted, judge! his charge, the crazy town,
Just managed to be hindered crashing down—
His last sound troops ranged—care observed to post
His best of the maimed soldiers innermost—
So much was plain enough, but somehow struck
Him not before. And now with this strange luck
Of Tito's news, rewarding his address
So well, what thought he of?—how the success
With Friedrich's rescript there would either hush
Old Ecelin's scruples, bring the manly flush
To his young son's white cheek, or, last, exempt
Himself from telling what there was to tempt?
[Sidenote: Resembling Sordello in nothing else.]
No: that this minstrel was Romano's last
Servant—himself the first! Could he contrast
The whole!—that minstrel's thirty years just spent
In doing naught, their notablest event
This morning's journey hither, as I told—
Who yet was lean, outworn and really old,
A stammering awkward man that scarce dared raise

His eye before the magisterial gaze—
And Salinguerra with his fears and hopes
Of sixty years, his Emperors and Popes,
Cares and contrivances, yet, you would say,
'T was a youth nonchalantly looked away
Through the embrasure northward o'er the sick
Expostulating trees—so agile, quick
[Sidenote: How he was made in body and spirit,]
And graceful turned the head on the broad chest
Encased in pliant steel, his constant vest,
Whence split the sun off in a spray of fire
Across the room; and, loosened of its tire
Of steel, that head let breathe the comely brown
Large massive locks discolored as if a crown
Encircled them, so frayed the basnet where
A sharp white line divided clean the hair;
Glossy above, glossy below, it swept
Curling and fine about a brow thus kept
Calm, laid coat upon coat, marble and sound:
This was the mystic mark the Tuscan found,
Mused of, turned over books about. Square-faced,
No lion more; two vivid eyes, enchased
In hollows filled with many a shade and streak
Settling from the bold nose and bearded cheek.
Nor might the half-smile reach them that deformed
A lip supremely perfect else—unwarmed,
Unwidened, less or more; indifferent
Whether on trees or men his thoughts were bent,
Thoughts rarely, after all, in trim and train
As now a period was fulfilled again:
Of such, a series made his life, compressed
In each, one story serving for the rest—
[Sidenote: And what had been his career of old.]
How his life-streams rolling arrived at last
At the barrier, whence, were it once overpast,
They would emerge, a river to the end,—
Gathered themselves up, paused, bade fate befriend,
Took the leap, hung a minute at the height,
Then fell back to oblivion infinite:
Therefore he smiled. Beyond stretched garden-grounds
Where late the adversary, breaking bounds,
Had gained him an occasion, That above,
That eagle, testified he could improve
Effectually. The Kaiser's symbol lay
Beside his rescript, a new badge by way
Of baldric; while,—another thing that marred
Alike emprise, achievement and reward,—
Ecelin's missive was conspicuous too.

What past life did those flying thoughts pursue?
As his, few names in Mantua half so old;

But at Ferrara, where his sires enrolled
It latterly, the Adelardi spared
No pains to rival them: both factions shared
Ferrara, so that, counted out, 't would yield
A product very like the city's shield,
Half black and white, or Ghibellin and Guelf
As after Salinguerra styled himself
And Este, who, till Marchesalla died,
(Last of the Adelardi)—never tried
His fortune there: with Marchesalla's child
Would pass—could Blacks and Whites be reconciled,
And young Taurello wed Linguetta—wealth
And sway to a sole grasp. Each treats by stealth
Already: when the Guelfs, the Ravennese
Arrive, assault the Pietro quarter, seize
Linguetta, and are gone! Men's first dismay
Abated somewhat, hurries down, to lay
The after indignation, Boniface,
This Richard's father. "Learn the full disgrace
Averted, ere you blame us Guelfs, who rate
Your Salinguerra, your sole potentate
That might have been, 'mongst Este's valvassors—
Ay, Azzo's—who, not privy to, abhors
Our step; but we were zealous." Azzo 's then
To do with! Straight a meeting of old men:
"Old Salinguerra dead, his heir a boy,
What if we change our ruler and decoy
The Lombard Eagle of the azure sphere
With Italy to build in, fix him here,
Settle the city's troubles in a trice?
For private wrong, let public good suffice!"
[Sidenote: The original check to his fortunes,]
In fine, young Salinguerra's stanchest friends
Talked of the townsmen making him amends,
Gave him a goshawk, and affirmed there was
Rare sport, one morning, over the green grass
A mile or so. He sauntered through the plain,
Was restless, fell to thinking, turned again
In time for Azzo's entry with the bride;
Count Boniface rode smirking at their side;
"She brings him half Ferrara," whispers flew,
"And all Ancona! If the stripling knew!"
Anon the stripling was in Sicily
Where Heinrich ruled in right of Constance; he
Was gracious nor his guest incapable;
Each understood the other. So it fell,
One Spring, when Azzo, thoroughly at ease,
Had near forgotten by what precise degrees
He crept at first to such a downy seat,
The Count trudged over in a special heat
To bid him of God's love dislodge from each

Of Salinguerra's palaces,—a breach
Might yawn else, not so readily to shut,
For who was just arrived at Mantua but
The youngster, sword on thigh and tuft on chin,
[Sidenote: Which he was in the way to retrieve,]
With tokens for Celano, Ecelin,
Pistore, and the like! Next news,—no whit
Do any of Ferrara's domes befit
His wife of Heinrich's very blood: a band
Of foreigners assemble, understand
Garden-constructing, level and surround,
Build up and bury in. A last news crowned
The consternation: since his infant's birth,
He only waits they end his wondrous girth
Of trees that link San Pietro with Tomà,
To visit Mantua. When the Podestà
Ecelin, at Vicenza, called his friend
Taurello thither, what could be their end
But to restore the Ghibellins' late Head,
The Kaiser helping? He with most to dread
From vengeance and reprisal, Azzo, there
With Boniface beforehand, as aware
Of plots in progress, gave alarm, expelled
Both plotters: but the Guelfs in triumph yelled
Too hastily. The burning and the flight,
And how Taurello, occupied that night
With Ecelin, lost wife and son, I told:
[Sidenote: When a fresh calamity destroyed all:]
—Not how he bore the blow, retained his hold,
Got friends safe through, left enemies the worst
O' the fray, and hardly seemed to care at first:
But afterward men heard not constantly
Of Salinguerra's House so sure to be!
Though Azzo simply gained by the event
A shifting of his plagues—the first, content
To fall behind the second and estrange
So far his nature, suffer such a change
That in Romano sought he wife and child
And for Romano's sake seemed reconciled
To losing individual life, which shrunk
As the other prospered—mortised in his trunk,
Like a dwarf palm which wanton Arabs foil
Of bearing its own proper wine and oil,
By grafting into it the stranger-vine,
Which sucks its heart out, sly and serpentine,
Till forth one vine-palm feathers to the root,
And red drops moisten the insipid fruit.
Once Adelaide set on,—the subtle mate
Of the weak soldier, urged to emulate
The Church's valiant women deed for deed,
And paragon her namesake, win the meed

O' the great Matilda,—soon they overbore
The rest of Lombardy,—not as before
By an instinctive truculence, but patched
The Kaiser's strategy until it matched
The Pontiff's, sought old ends by novel means.
"Only, why is it Salinguerra screens
Himself behind Romano?—him we bade
Enjoy our shine i' the front, not seek the shade!"
—Asked Heinrich, somewhat of the tardiest
To comprehend. Nor Philip acquiesced
At once in the arrangement; reasoned, plied
His friend with offers of another bride,
A statelier function—fruitlessly: 't was plain
[Sidenote: He sank into a secondary personage,]
Taurello through some weakness must remain
Obscure. And Otho, free to judge of both,
—Ecelin the unready, harsh and loth,
And this more plausible and facile wight
With every point a-sparkle—chose the right,
Admiring how his predecessors harped
On the wrong man: "thus," quoth he, "wits are warped
By outsides!" Carelessly, meanwhile, his life
Suffered its many turns of peace and strife
In many lands—you hardly could surprise
The man; who shamed Sordello (recognize!)
In this as much beside, that, unconcerned
What qualities were natural or earned,
With no ideal of graces, as they came
He took them, singularly well the same—
Speaking the Greek's own language, just because
Your Greek eludes you, leave the least of flaws
In contracts with him; while, since Arab lore
Holds the stars' secret—take one trouble more
And master it! 'Tis done, and now deter
Who may the Tuscan, once Jove trined for her,
From Friedrich's path!—Friedrich, whose pilgrimage
The same man puts aside, whom he'll engage
To leave next year John Brienne in the lurch,
Come to Bassano, see Saint Francis' church
And judge of Guido the Bolognian's piece
Which, lend Taurello credit, rivals Greece—
Angels, with aureoles like golden quoits
Pitched home, applauding Ecelin's exploits.
For elegance, he strung the angelot,
[Sidenote: With the appropriate graces of such.]
Made rhymes thereto; for prowess, clove he not
Tiso, last siege, from crest to crupper? Why
Detail you thus a varied mastery
But to show how Taurello, on the watch
For men, to read their hearts and thereby catch
Their capabilities and purposes,

Displayed himself so far as displayed these:
While our Sordello only cared to know
About men as a means whereby he'd show
Himself, and men had much or little worth
According as they kept in or drew forth
That self; the other's choicest instruments
Surmised him shallow.

Meantime, malcontents
Dropped off, town after town grew wiser. "How
Change the world's face?" asked people; "as 't is now
It has been, will be ever: very fine
Subjecting things profane to things divine,
In talk! This contumacy will fatigue
The vigilance of Este and the League!
The Ghibellins gain on us!"—as it happed.
Old Azzo and old Boniface, entrapped
By Ponte Alto, both in one month's space
Slept at Verona: either left a brace
Of sons—but, three years after, either's pair
Lost Guglielm and Aldobrand its heir:
Azzo remained and Richard—all the stay
Of Este and Saint Boniface, at bay
[Sidenote: But Ecelin, he set in front, falling,]
As 't were. Then, either Ecelin grew old
Or his brain altered—not o' the proper mould
For new appliances—his old palm-stock
Endured no influx of strange strengths. He'd rock
As in a drunkenness, or chuckle low
As proud of the completeness of his woe,
Then weep real tears;—now make some mad onslaught
On Este, heedless of the lesson taught
So painfully,—now cringe for peace, sue peace
At price of past gain, bar of fresh increase
To the fortunes of Romano. Up at last
Rose Este, down Romano sank as fast.
And men remarked these freaks of peace and war
Happened while Salinguerra was afar:
Whence every friend besought him, all in vain,
To use his old adherent's wits again.
Not he!—"who had advisers in his sons,
Could plot himself, nor needed any one's
Advice." 'T was Adelaide's remaining stanch
Prevented his destruction root and branch
Forthwith; but when she died, doom fell, for gay
He made alliances, gave lands away
To whom it pleased accept them, and withdrew
Forever from the world. Taurello, who
Was summoned to the convent, then refused
A word at the wicket, patience thus abused,
Promptly threw off alike his imbecile

Ally's yoke, and his own frank, foolish smile.
Soon a few movements of the happier sort
Changed matters, put himself in men's report
As heretofore; he had to fight, beside,
And that became him ever. So, in pride
[Sidenote: Salinguerra must again come forward,]
And flushing of this kind of second youth,
He dealt a good-will blow. Este in truth
Lay prone—and men remembered, somewhat late,
A laughing old outrageous stifled hate
He bore to Este—how it would outbreak
At times spite of disguise, like an earthquake
In sunny weather—as that noted day
When with his hundred friends he tried to slay
Azzo before the Kaiser's face: and how,
On Azzo's calm refusal to allow
A liegeman's challenge, straight he too was calmed:
As if his hate could bear to lie embalmed,
Bricked up, the moody Pharaoh, and survive
All intermediate crumblings, to arrive
At earth's catastrophe—'t was Este's crash,
Not Azzo's he demanded, so, no rash
Procedure! Este's true antagonist
Rose out of Ecelin: all voices whist,
All eyes were sharpened, wits predicted. He
'T was, leaned in the embrasure absently,
[Sidenote: Why and how, is let out in soliloquy.]
Amused with his own efforts, now, to trace
With his steel-sheathed forefinger Friedrich's face
I' the dust: but as the trees waved sere, his smile
Deepened, and words expressed its thought erewhile.
"Ay, fairly housed at last, my old compeer?
That we should stick together, all the year
I kept Vicenza!—How old Boniface,
Old Azzo caught us in its market-place,
He by that pillar, I at this,—caught each
In mid swing, more than fury of his speech,
Egging the rabble on to disavow
Allegiance to their Marquis—Bacchus, how
They boasted! Ecelin must turn their drudge,
Nor, if released, will Salinguerra grudge
Paying arrears of tribute due long since—
Bacchus! My man could promise then, nor wince,
The bones-and-muscles! Sound of wind and limb,
Spoke he the set excuse I framed for him:
And now he sits me, slavering and mute,
Intent on chafing each starved purple foot
Benumbed past aching with the altar slab—
Will no vein throb there when some monk shall blab
Spitefully to the circle of bald scalps,
[Sidenote: Ecelin, he did all for, is a monk now,]

'Friedrich's affirmed to be our side the Alps'
—Eh, brother Lactance, brother Anaclet?
Sworn to abjure the world, its fume and fret,
God's own now? Drop the dormitory bar,
Enfold the scanty gray serge scapular
Twice o'er the cowl to muffle memories out!
So! But the midnight whisper turns a shout,
Eyes wink, mouths open, pulses circulate
In the stone walls: the past, the world you hate
Is with you, ambush, open field—or see
The surging flame—we fire Vicenza—glee!
Follow, let Pilio and Bernardo chafe!
Bring up the Mantuans—through San Biagio—safe!
Ah, the mad people waken? Ah, they writhe
And reach us? If they block the gate? No tithe
Can pass—keep back, you Bassanese! The edge,
Use the edge—shear, thrust, hew, melt down the wedge,
Let out the black of those black upturned eyes!
Hell—are they sprinkling fire too? The blood fries
And hisses on your brass gloves as they tear
Those upturned faces choking with despair.
Brave! Slidder through the reeking gate! 'How now?
You six had charge of her?' And then the vow
Comes, and the foam spirts, hair's plucked, till one shriek
(I hear it) and you fling—you cannot speak—
Your gold-flowered basnet to a man who haled
The Adelaide he dared scarce view unveiled
This morn, naked across the fire: how crown
The archer that exhausted lays you down
Your infant, smiling at the flame, and dies?
While one, while mine ...

"Bacchus! I think there lies
More than one corpse there" (and he paced the room)
"—Another cinder somewhere: 't was my doom
Beside, my doom! If Adelaide is dead,
I live the same, this Azzo lives instead
Of that to me, and we pull, any how,
Este into a heap: the matter's now
[Sidenote: *Just when the prize awaits somebody;*]
At the true juncture slipping us so oft.
Ay, Heinrich died and Otho, please you doffed
His crown at such a juncture! Still, if holds
Our Friedrich's purpose, if this chain enfolds
The neck of ... who but this same Ecelin
That must recoil when the best days begin!
Recoil? that's naught; if the recoiler leaves
His name for me to fight with, no one grieves:
But he must interfere, forsooth, unlock
His cloister to become my stumbling-block
Just as of old! Ay, ay, there 't is again—

The land's inevitable Head—explain
The reverences that subject us! Count
These Ecelins now! Not to say as fount,
Originating power of thought,—from twelve
That drop i' the trenches they joined hands to delve,
Six shall surpass him, but ... why, men must twine
Somehow with something! Ecelin's a fine
[Sidenote: Himself, if it were only worth while,]
Clear name! 'T were simpler, doubtless, twine with me
At once our cloistered friend's capacity
Was of a sort! I had to share myself
In fifty portions, like an o'ertasked elf
That's forced illume in fifty points the vast
Rare vapor he's environed by. At last
My strengths, though sorely frittered, e'en converge
And crown ... no, Bacchus, they have yet to urge
The man be crowned!

"That aloe, an he durst,
Would climb! Just such a bloated sprawler first
I noted in Messina's castle-court
The day I came, when Heinrich asked in sport
If I would pledge my faith to win him back
His right in Lombardy: 'for, once bid pack
Marauders,' he continued, 'in my stead
You rule, Taurello!' and upon this head
Laid the silk glove of Constance—I see her
Too, mantled head to foot in miniver,
Retrude following!

"I am absolved
From further toil: the empery devolved
On me, 't was Tito's word: I have to lay
For once my plan, pursue my plan my way,
Prompt nobody, and render an account
Taurello to Taurello! Nay, I mount
To Friedrich: he conceives the post I kept,
—Who did true service, able or inept,
Who's worthy guerdon, Ecelin or I.
Me guerdoned, counsel follows: would he vie
With the Pope really? Azzo, Boniface
Compose a right-arm Hohenstauffen's race
Must break ere govern Lombardy. I point
How easy 't were to twist, once out of joint,
The socket from the bone: my Azzo's stare
Meanwhile! for I, this idle strap to wear,
Shall—fret myself abundantly, what end
To serve? There's left me twenty years to spend
[Sidenote: As it may be—but also, as it may not be—]
—How better than my old way? Had I one
Who labored to o'erthrow my work—a son

Hatching with Azzo superb treachery,
To root my pines up and then poison me,
Suppose—'t were worth while frustrate that! Beside,
Another life's ordained me: the world's tide
Rolls, and what hope of parting from the press
Of waves, a single wave through weariness
Gently lifted aside, laid upon shore?
My life must be lived out in foam and roar,
No question. Fifty years the province held
Taurello; troubles raised, and troubles quelled,
He in the midst—who leaves this quaint stone place,
These trees a year or two, then not a trace
Of him! How obtain hold, fetter men's tongues
Like this poor minstrel with the foolish songs—
To which, despite our bustle, he is linked?
—Flowers one may tease, that never grow extinct.
Ay, that patch, surely, green as ever, where
I set Her Moorish lentisk, by the stair,
To overawe the aloes; and we trod
Those flowers, how call you such?—into the sod;
A stately foreigner—a world of pain
To make it thrive, arrest rough winds—all vain!
It would decline; these would not he destroyed:
And now, where is it? where can you avoid
The flowers? I frighten children twenty years
Longer!—which way, too, Ecelin appears
To thwart me, for his son's besotted youth
Gives promise of the proper tiger-tooth:
They feel it at Vicenza! Fate, fate, fate,
My fine Taurello! Go you, promulgate
Friedrich's decree, and here 's shall aggrandize
Young Ecelin—your Prefect's badge! a prize
[Sidenote: The supposition he most inclines to;]
Too precious, certainly.

"How now? Compete
With my old comrade? shuffle from their seat
His children? Paltry dealing! Don't I know
Ecelin? now, I think, and years ago!
What's changed—the weakness? did not I compound
For that, and undertake to keep him sound
Despite it? Here's Taurello hankering
After a boy's preferment—this plaything
To carry, Bacchus!" And he laughed.

Remark
Why schemes wherein cold-blooded men embark
Prosper, when your enthusiastic sort
Fail: while these last are ever stopping short—
(So much they should—so little they can do!)
The careless tribe see nothing to pursue

If they desist; meantime their scheme succeeds.
Thoughts were caprices in the course of deeds
Methodic with Taurello; so, he turned,
Enough amused by fancies fairly earned
Of Este's horror-struck submitted neck,
And Richard, the cowed braggart, at his beck,
[Sidenote: Being contented with mere vengeance.]
To his own petty but immediate doubt
If he could pacify the League without
Conceding Richard; just to this was brought
That interval of vain discursive thought!
As, shall I say, some Ethiop, past pursuit
Of all enslavers, dips a shackled foot
Burnt to the blood, into the drowsy black
Enormous watercourse which guides him back
To his own tribe again, where he is king;
And laughs because he guesses, numbering
The yellower poison-wattles on the pouch
Of the first lizard wrested from its couch
Under the slime (whose skin, the while he strips
To cure his nostril with, and festered lips,
And eyeballs bloodshot through the desert-blast)
That he has reached its boundary, at last
May breathe;—thinks o'er enchantments of the South
Sovereign to plague his enemies, their mouth,
Eyes, nails, and hair; but, these enchantments tried
In fancy, puts them soberly aside
For truth, projects a cool return with friends,
The likelihood of winning mere amends
Ere long; thinks that, takes comfort silently,
Then, from the river's brink, his wrongs and he,
Hugging revenge close to their hearts, are soon
Off-striding for the Mountains of the Moon.
Midnight: the watcher nodded on his spear,
Since clouds dispersing left a passage clear
For any meagre and discolored moon
To venture forth; and such was peering soon
Above the harassed city—her close lanes
Closer, not half so tapering her fanes,
As though she shrunk into herself to keep
What little life was saved, more safely. Heap
By heap the watch-fires mouldered, and beside
The blackest spoke Sordello and replied
Palma with none to listen. "'T is your cause:
[Sidenote: Sordello, taught what Ghibellins are,]
What makes a Ghibellin? There should be laws—
(Remember how my youth escaped! I trust
To you for manhood, Palma; tell me just
As any child)—there must be laws at work
Explaining this. Assure me, good may lurk
Under the bad,—my multitude has part

In your designs, their welfare is at heart
With Salinguerra, to their interest
Refer the deeds he dwelt on,—so divest
Our conference of much that scared me. Why
Affect that heartless tone to Tito? I
Esteemed myself, yes, in my inmost mind
This morn, a recreant to my race—mankind
O'erlooked till now: why boast my spirit's force,
—Such force denied its object? why divorce
These, then admire my spirit's flight the same
As though it bore up, helped some half-orbed flame
Else quenched in the dead void, to living space?
That orb cast off to chaos and disgrace,
Why vaunt so much my unencumbered dance,
Making a feat's facilities enhance
Its marvel? But I front Taurello, one
Of happier fate, and all I should have done,
He does; the people's good being paramount
With him, their progress may perhaps account
For his abiding still; whereas you heard
The talk with Tito—the excuse preferred
For burning those five hostages,—and broached
By way of blind, as you and I approached,
I do believe."

She spoke: then he, "My thought
Plainlier expressed! All to your profit—naught
Meantime of these, of conquests to achieve
For them, of wretchedness he might relieve
[Sidenote: And what Guelfs, approves of neither.]
While profiting your party. Azzo, too,
Supports a cause: what cause? Do Guelfs pursue
Their ends by means like yours, or better?"

When
The Guelfs were proved alike, men weighed with men,
And deed with deed, blaze, blood, with blood and blaze,
Morn broke: "Once more, Sordello, meet its gaze
Proudly—the people's charge against thee fails
In every point, while either party quails!
These are the busy ones: be silent thou!
Two parties take the world up, and allow
No third, yet have one principle, subsist
By the same injustice; whoso shall enlist
With either, ranks with man's inveterate foes.
So there is one less quarrel to compose:
The Guelf, the Ghibellin may be to curse—
I have done nothing, but both sides do worse
Than nothing. Nay, to me, forgotten, reft
Of insight, lapped by trees and flowers, was left
The notion of a service—ha? What lured

Me here, what mighty aim was I assured
Must move Taurello? What if there remained
[Sidenote: Have men a cause distinct from both?]
A cause, intact, distinct from these, ordained
For me, its true discoverer?"

Some one pressed
Before them here, a watcher, to suggest
The subject for a ballad: "They must know
The tale of the dead worthy, long ago
Consul of Rome—that 's long ago for us,
Minstrels and bowmen, idly squabbling thus
In the world's corner—but too late no doubt,
For the brave time he sought to bring about.
[Sidenote: Who was the famed Roman Crescentius?]
—Not know Crescentius Nomentanus?" Then
He cast about for terms to tell him, when
Sordello disavowed it, how they used
Whenever their Superior introduced
A novice to the Brotherhood—("for I
Was just a brown-sleeve brother, merrily
Appointed too," quoth he, "till Innocent
Bade me relinquish, to my small content,
My wife or my brown sleeves")—some brother spoke
Ere nocturns of Crescentius, to revoke
The edict issued, after his demise,
Which blotted fame alike and effigies,
All out except a floating power, a name
Including, tending to produce the same
Great act. Rome, dead, forgotten, lived at least
Within that brain, though to a vulgar priest
And a vile stranger,—two not worth a slave
Of Rome's, Pope John, King Otho,—fortune gave
The rule there: so, Crescentius, haply dressed
In white, called Roman Consul for a jest,
Taking the people at their word, forth stepped
As upon Brutus' heel, nor ever kept
Rome waiting,—stood erect, and from his brain
Gave Rome out on its ancient place again,
Ay, bade proceed with Brutus' Rome, Kings styled
Themselves mere citizens of, and, beguiled
Into great thoughts thereby, would choose the gem
Out of a lapfull, spoil their diadem
—The Senate's cypher was so hard to scratch!
He flashes like a phanal, all men catch
The flame, Rome 's just accomplished! when returned
Otho, with John, the Consul's step had spurned,
And Hugo Lord of Este, to redress
The wrongs of each. Crescentius in the stress
Of adverse fortune bent. "They crucified
Their Consul in the Forum; and abide

E'er since such slaves at Rome, that I—(for I
Was once a brown-sleeve brother, merrily
Appointed)—I had option to keep wife
Or keep brown sleeves, and managed in the strife
Lose both. A song of Rome!"

And Rome, indeed,
Robed at Goito in fantastic weed,
The Mother-City of his Mantuan days,
Looked an established point of light whence rays
Traversed the world; for, all the clustered homes
Beside of men, seemed bent on being Romes
In their degree; the question was, how each
Should most resemble Rome, clean out of reach.
[Sidenote: How if, in the reintegration of Rome,]
Nor, of the Two, did either principle
Struggle to change—but to possess—Rome, still,
Guelf Rome or Ghibellin Rome.

Let Rome advance!
Rome, as she struck Sordello's ignorance—
How could he doubt one moment? Rome 's the Cause!
Rome of the Pandects, all the world's new laws—
Of the Capitol, of Castle Angelo;
New structures, that inordinately glow,
Subdued, brought back to harmony, made ripe
By many a relic of the archetype
Extant for wonder; every upstart church
That hoped to leave old temples in the lurch,
Corrected by the Theatre forlorn
That,—as a mundane shell, its world late born,—
Lay and o'ershadowed it. These hints combined,
[Sidenote: Be typified the triumph of mankind?]
Rome typifies the scheme to put mankind
Once more in full possession of their rights.
"Let us have Rome again! On me it lights
To build up Rome—on me, the first and last:
For such a future was endured the past!"
And thus, in the gray twilight, forth he sprung
To give his thought consistency among
The very People—let their facts avail
Finish the dream grown from the archer's tale.

BOOK THE FIFTH

Is it the same Sordello in the dusk
As at the dawn?—merely a perished husk
Now, that arose a power fit to build
[Sidenote: Mankind triumph of a sudden?]

Up Rome again? The proud conception chilled
So soon? Ay, watch that latest dream of thine—A
Rome indebted to no Palatine—
Drop arch by arch, Sordello! Art possessed
Of thy wish now, rewarded for thy quest
To-day among Ferrara's squalid sons?
Are this and this and this the shining ones
Meet for the Shining City? Sooth to say,
Your favored tenantry pursue their way
After a fashion! This companion slips
On the smooth causey, t' other blinkard trips
At his mooned sandal. "Leave to lead the brawls
Here i' the atria?" No, friend! He that sprawls
On aught but a stibadium ... what his dues
Who puts the lustral vase to such an use?
Oh, huddle up the day's disasters! March,
Ye runagates, and drop thou, arch by arch,
Rome!

Yet before they quite disband—a whim—
Study mere shelter, now, for him, and him,
Nay, even the worst,—just house them! Any cave
Suffices: throw out earth! A loophole? Brave!
They ask to feel the sun shine, see the grass
Grow, hear the larks sing? Dead art thou, alas,
And I am dead! But here's our son excels
At hurdle-weaving any Scythian, fells
Oak and devises rafters, dreams and shapes
His dream into a door-post, just escapes
The mystery of hinges. Lie we both
Perdue another age. The goodly growth
Of brick and stone! Our building-pelt was rough,
But that descendant's garb suits well enough
A portico-contriver. Speed the years—
[Sidenote: Why, the work should be one of ages,]
What's time to us? At last, a city rears
Itself! nay, enter—what's the grave to us?
Lo, our forlorn acquaintance carry thus
The head! Successively sewer, forum, cirque—
Last age, an aqueduct was counted work,
But now they tire the artificer upon
Blank alabaster, black obsidion,
—Careful, Jove's face be duly fulgurant,
And mother Venus' kiss-creased nipples pant
Back into pristine pulpiness, ere fixed
Above the baths. What difference betwixt
This Rome and ours—resemblance what, between
That scurvy dumb-show and this pageant sheen—
These Romans and our rabble? Use thy wit!
The work marched: step by step,—a workman fit
Took each, nor too fit,—to one task, one time,—

No leaping o'er the petty to the prime,
[Sidenote: If performed equally and thoroughly;]
When just the substituting osier lithe
For brittle bulrush, sound wood for soft withe,
To further loam-and-roughcast-work a stage,—
Exacts an architect, exacts an age:
No tables of the Mauritanian tree
For men whose maple log 's their luxury!
That way was Rome built. "Better" (say you) "merge
At once all workmen in the demiurge,
All epochs in a lifetime, every task
In one!" So should the sudden city bask
I' the day—while those we'd feast there, want the knack
Of keeping fresh-chalked gowns from speck and brack,
Distinguish not rare peacock from vile swan,
Nor Mareotic juice from Cæcuban.
"Enough of Rome! 'T was happy to conceive
Rome on a sudden, nor shall fate bereave
Me of that credit: for the rest, her spite
Is an old story—serves my folly right
By adding yet another to the dull
List of abortions—things proved beautiful
Could they be done, Sordello cannot do."

He sat upon the terrace, plucked and threw
The powdery aloe-cusps away, saw shift
Rome's walls, and drop arch after arch, and drift
Mist-like afar those pillars of all stripe,
Mounds of all majesty. "Thou archetype,
Last of my dreams and loveliest, depart!"
And then a low voice wound into his heart:
"Sordello!" (low as some old Pythoness
Conceding to a Lydian King's distress
The cause of his long error—one mistake
Of her past oracle) "Sordello, wake!
God has conceded two sights to a man—
[Sidenote: And a man can do but a man's portion.]
One, of men's whole work, time's completed plan,
The other, of the minute's work, man's first
Step to the plan's completeness: what's dispersed
Save hope of that supreme step which, descried
Earliest, was meant still to remain untried
Only to give you heart to take your own
Step, and there stay—leaving the rest alone?
Where is the vanity? Why count as one
The first step, with the last step? What is gone
Except Rome's aëry magnificence,
That last step you'd take first?—an evidence
You were God: be man now! Let those glances fall!
The basis, the beginning step of all,
Which proves you just a man—is that gone too?

Pity to disconcert one versed as you
In fate's ill-nature! but its full extent
Eludes Sordello, even: the veil rent,
Read the black writing—that collective man
Outstrips the individual! Who began

[Sidenote: The last of each series of workmen]

The acknowledged greatnesses? Ay, your own art
Shall serve us: put the poet's mimes apart—
Close with the poet's self, and lo, a dim
Yet too plain form divides itself from him!
Alcamo's song enmeshes the lulled Isle,
Woven into the echoes left erewhile
By Nina, one soft web of song: no more
Turning his name, then, flower-like o'er and o'er!
An elder poet in the younger's place;
Nina's the strength, but Alcamo's the grace:
Each neutralizes each then! Search your fill;
You get no whole and perfect Poet—still
New Ninas, Alcamos, till time's midnight
Shrouds all—or better say, the shutting light
Of a forgotten yesterday. Dissect
Every ideal workman—(to reject
In favor of your fearful ignorance
The thousand phantasms eager to advance,

[Sidenote: Sums up in himself all predecessors.]

And point you but to those within your reach)—
Were you the first who brought—(in modern speech)
The Multitude to be materialized?
That loose eternal unrest—who devised
An apparition i' the midst? The rout
Was cheeked, a breathless ring was formed about
That sudden flower: get round at any risk
The gold-rough pointel, silver-blazing disk
O' the lily! Swords across it! Reign thy reign

[Sidenote: We just see Charlemagne, Hildebrand,]

And serve thy frolic service, Charlemagne!
—The very child of over-joyousness,
Unfeeling thence, strong therefore: Strength by stress
Of Strength comes of that forehead confident,
Those widened eyes expecting heart's content,
A calm as out of just-quelled noise; nor swerves
For doubt, the ample cheek in gracious curves
Abutting on the upthrust nether lip:
He wills, how should he doubt then? Ages slip:
Was it Sordello pried into the work
So far accomplished, and discovered lurk
A company amid the other clans,
Only distinct in priests for castellans
And popes for suzerains (their rule confessed
Its rule, their interest its interest,
Living for sake of living—there an end,—

Wrapt in itself, no energy to spend
In making adversaries or allies),—
Dived you into its capabilities
And dared create, out of that sect, a soul
Should turn a multitude, already whole,
Into its body? Speak plainer! Is 't so sure
God's church lives by a King's investiture?
Look to last step! A staggering—a shock—
What's mere sand is demolished, while the rock
Endures: a column of black fiery dust
Blots heaven—that help was prematurely thrust
Aside, perchance!—but air clears, naught's erased
Of the true outline! Thus much being firm based,
The other was a scaffold. See him stand
Buttressed upon his mattock, Hildebrand
Of the huge brain-mask welded ply o'er ply
As in a forge; it buries either eye
White and extinct, that stupid brow; teeth clenched,
The neck tight-corded, too, the chin deep-trenched,
As if a cloud enveloped him while fought
Under its shade, grim prizers, thought with thought
At dead-lock, agonizing he, until
The victor thought leap radiant up, and Will,
The slave with folded arms and drooping lids
They fought for, lean forth flame-like as it bids.
Call him no flower—a mandrake of the earth,
Thwarted and dwarfed and blasted in its birth,
Rather,—a fruit of suffering's excess,
Thence feeling, therefore stronger: still by stress
Of Strength, work Knowledge! Full three hundred years
Have men to wear away in smiles and tears
Between the two that nearly seemed to touch,
[Sidenote: In composite work they end and name.]
Observe you! quit one workman and you clutch
Another, letting both their trains go by—
The actors-out of either's policy,
Heinrich, on this hand, Otho, Barbaross,
Carry the three Imperial crowns across,
Aix' Iron, Milan's Silver, and Rome's Gold—
While Alexander, Innocent uphold
On that, each Papal key—but, link on link,
Why is it neither chain betrays a chink?
How coalesce the small and great? Alack,
For one thrust forward, fifty such fall back!
Do the popes coupled there help Gregory
Alone? Hark—from the hermit Peter's cry
At Claremont, down to the first serf that says
Friedrich 's no liege of his while he delays
Getting the Pope's curse off him! The Crusade—
Or trick of breeding Strength by other aid
Than Strength, is safe. Hark—from the wild harangue

Of Vimmercato, to the carroch's clang
Yonder! The League—or trick of turning Strength
Against Pernicious Strength, is safe at length.
Yet hark—from Mantuan Albert making cease
The fierce ones, to Saint Francis preaching peace
Yonder! God's Truce—or trick to supersede
The very Use of Strength, is safe. Indeed
We trench upon the future. Who is found
To take next step, next age—trail o'er the ground—
Shall I say, gourd-like?—not the flower's display
Nor the root's prowess, but the plenteous way
O' the plant—produced by joy and sorrow, whence
Unfeeling and yet feeling, strongest thence?
Knowledge by stress of merely Knowledge? No—
E'en were Sordello ready to forego
His life for this, 't were overleaping work
Some one has first to do, howe'er it irk,
Nor stray a foot's breadth from the beaten road.
Who means to help must still support the load
Hildebrand lifted—'why hast Thou,' he groaned,
'Imposed on me a burden, Paul had moaned,
And Moses dropped beneath?' Much done—and yet
Doubtless that grandest task God ever set
On man, left much to do: at his arm's wrench,
Charlemagne's scaffold fell; but pillars blench
Merely, start back again—perchance have been
Taken for buttresses: crash every screen,
Hammer the tenons better, and engage
A gang about your work, for the next age
Or two, of Knowledge, part by Strength and part
By Knowledge! Then, indeed, perchance may start
Sordello on his race—would time divulge
Such secrets! If one step's awry, one bulge
Calls for correction by a step we thought
Got over long since, why, till that is wrought,
No progress! And the scaffold in its turn
Becomes, its service o'er, a thing to spurn.
Meanwhile, if your half-dozen years of life
In store dispose you to forego the strife,
Who takes exception? Only bear in mind,
Ferrara's reached, Goito 's left behind:
[Sidenote: If associates trouble you, stand off!]
As you then were, as half yourself, desist!
—The warrior-part of you may, an it list,
Finding real falchions difficult to poise,
Fling them afar and taste the cream of joys
By wielding such in fancy,—what is bard
Of you may spurn the vehicle that marred
Elys so much, and in free fancy glut
His sense, yet write no verses—you have but
To please yourself for law, and once could please

What once appeared yourself, by dreaming these
Rather than doing these, in days gone by.
But all is changed the moment you descry
Mankind as half yourself,—then, fancy's trade
Ends once and always: how may half evade
The other half? men are found half of you.
Out of a thousand helps, just one or two
Can be accomplished presently: but flinch
From these (as from the falchion, raised an inch,
Elys, described a couplet) and make proof
Of fancy,—then, while one half lolls aloof
I' the vines, completing Rome to the tip-top—
See if, for that, your other half will stop

[Sidenote: Should the new sympathies allow you.]

A tear, begin a smile! The rabble's woes,
Ludicrous in their patience as they chose
To sit about their town and quietly
Be slaughtered,—the poor reckless soldiery,
With their ignoble rhymes on Richard, how
'Polt-foot,' sang they, 'was in a pitfall now,'
Cheering each other from the engine-mounts,—
That crippled sprawling idiot who recounts
How, lopped of limbs, he lay, stupid as stone,
Till the pains crept from out him one by one,
And wriggles round the archers on his head
To earn a morsel of their chestnut bread,—
And Cino, always in the self-same place
Weeping; beside that other wretch's case,
Eyepits to ear, one gangrene since he plied
The engine in his coat of raw sheep's hide
A double watch in the noon sun; and see
Lucchino, beauty, with the favors free,
Trim hacqueton, spruce heard and scented hair,
Campaigning it for the first time—cut there
In two already, boy enough to crawl
For latter orpine round the southern wall,
Tomà, where Richard's kept, because that whore
Marfisa, the fool never saw before,
Sickened for flowers this wearisomest siege:
And Tiso's wife—men liked their pretty liege,
Cared for her least of whims once,—Berta, wed
A twelvemonth gone, and, now poor Tiso's dead,
Delivering herself of his first child
On that chance heap of wet filth, reconciled
To fifty gazers!"—(Here a wind below
Made moody music augural of woe
From the pine barrier)—"What if, now the scene
Draws to a close, yourself have really been

[Sidenote: Time having been lost, choose quick!]

—You, plucking purples in Goito's moss
Like edges of a trabea (not to cross

Your consul-humor) or dry aloe-shafts
For fasces, at Ferrara—he, fate wafts,
This very age, her whole inheritance
Of opportunities? Yet you advance
Upon the last! Since talking is your trade,
There 's Salinguerra left you to persuade:
Fail! then"—

"No—no—which latest chance secure!"
Leaped up and cried Sordello: "this made sure,
The past were yet redeemable; its work
Was—help the Guelfs, whom I, howe'er it irk,
Thus help!" He shook the foolish aloe-haulm
[Sidenote: He takes his first step as a Guelf;]
Out of his doublet, paused, proceeded calm
To the appointed presence. The large head
Turned on its socket; "And your spokesman," said
The large voice, "is Elcorte's happy sprout?
Few such"—(so finishing a speech no doubt
Addressed to Palma, silent at his side)
"—My sober councils have diversified.
Elcorte's son! good: forward as you may,
Our lady's minstrel with so much to say!"
The hesitating sunset floated back,
Rosily traversed in the wonted track
The chamber, from the lattice o'er the girth
Of pines, to the huge eagle blacked in earth
Opposite,—outlined sudden, spur to crest,
That solid Salinguerra, and caressed
Palma's contour; 't was day looped back night's pall;
Sordello had a chance left spite of all.
And much he made of the convincing speech
Meant to compensate for the past and reach
Through his youth's daybreak of unprofit, quite
To his noon's labor, so proceed till night
Leisurely! The great argument to bind
Taurello with the Guelf Cause, body and mind,
—Came the consummate rhetoric to that?
Yet most Sordello's argument dropped flat
Through his accustomed fault of breaking yoke,
Disjoining him who felt from him who spoke.
Was 't not a touching incident—so prompt
A rendering the world its just accompt,
Once proved its debtor? Who'd suppose, before
This proof, that he, Goito's god of yore,
At duty's instance could demean himself
So memorably, dwindle to a Guelf?
Be sure, in such delicious flattery steeped,
His inmost self at the out-portion peeped,
Thus occupied; then stole a glance at those
Appealed to, curious if her color rose

Or his lip moved, while he discreetly urged
The need of Lombardy becoming purged
At soonest of her barons; the poor part
Abandoned thus, missing the blood at heart
And spirit in brain, unseasonably off
Elsewhere! But, though his speech was worthy scoff,
Good-humored Salinguerra, famed for tact
And tongue, who, careless of his phrase, ne'er lacked
The right phrase, and harangued Honorius dumb
At his accession,—looked as all fell plumb
To purpose and himself found interest
In every point his new instructor pressed
—Left playing with the rescript's white wax seal
To scrutinize Sordello head and heel.
He means to yield assent sure? No, alas!
All he replied was, "What, it comes to pass
That poesy, sooner than politics,
Makes fade young hair?" To think such speech could fix
Taurello!

Then a flash of bitter truth:
So fantasies could break and fritter youth
That he had long ago lost earnestness,
Lost will to work, lost power to express
[Sidenote: But to will and to do are different:]
The need of working! Earth was turned a grave:
No more occasions now, though he should crave
Just one, in right of superhuman toil,
To do what was undone, repair such spoil,
Alter the past—nothing would give the chance!
Not that he was to die; he saw askance
Protract the ignominious years beyond
To dream in—time to hope and time despond,
Remember and forget, be sad, rejoice
As saved a trouble; he might, at his choice,
One way or other, idle life out, drop
[Sidenote: He may sleep on the bed he has made.]
No few smooth verses by the way—for prop,
A thyrsus, these sad people, all the same,
Should pick up, and set store by,—far from blame,
Plant o'er his hearse, convinced his better part
Survived him. "Rather tear men out the heart
O' the truth!"—Sordello muttered, and renewed
His propositions for the Multitude.
But Salinguerra, who at this attack
Had thrown great breast and ruffling corselet back
To hear the better, smilingly resumed
His task; beneath, the carroch's warning boomed;
He must decide with Tito; courteously
He turned then, even seeming to agree
With his admonisher—"Assist the Pope,

Extend Guelf domination, fill the scope
O' the Church, thus based on All, by All, for All—
Change Secular to Evangelical"—
Echoing his very sentence: all seemed lost,
When suddenly he looked up, laughingly almost,
To Palma: "This opinion of your friend's—
For instance, would it answer Palma's ends?
Best, were it not, turn Guelf, submit our Strength"—
(Here he drew out his baldric to its length)
—"To the Pope's Knowledge—let our captive slip,
Wide to the walls throw ope our gates, equip
Azzo with ... what I hold here! Who'll subscribe
To a trite censure of the minstrel tribe
Henceforward? or pronounce, as Heinrich used,
'Spear-heads for battle, burr-heads for the joust!'
—When Constance, for his couplets, would promote
Alcamo, from a parti-colored coat,
To holding her lord's stirrup in the wars.
Not that I see where couplet-making jars
With common sense: at Mantua I had borne
This chanted, better than their most forlorn
Of bull-baits,—that's indisputable!"

Brave!
Whom vanity nigh slew, contempt shall save!
All's at an end: a Troubadour suppose
Mankind will class him with their friends or foes?
[Sidenote: Scorn flings cold water in his face,]
A puny uncouth ailing vassal think
The world and him bound in some special link?
Abrupt the visionary tether burst.
What were rewarded here, or what amerced
If a poor drudge, solicitous to dream
Deservingly, got tangled by his theme
So far as to conceit the knack or gift
Or whatsoe'er it be, of verse, might lift
The globe, a lever like the hand and head
Of—"Men of Action," as the Jongleurs said,
—"The Great Men," in the people's dialect?
And not a moment did this scorn affect
[Sidenote: Arouses him at last, to some purpose,]
Sordello: scorn the poet? They, for once,
Asking "what was," obtained a full response.
Bid Naddo think at Mantua, he had but
To look into his promptuary, put
Finger on a set thought in a set speech:
But was Sordello fitted thus for each
Conjecture? Nowise; since within his soul,
Perception brooded unexpressed and whole.
A healthy spirit like a healthy frame
Craves aliment in plenty—all the same,

Changes, assimilates its aliment.
Perceived Sordello, on a truth intent?
Next day no formularies more you saw
Than figs or olives in a sated maw.
'T is Knowledge, whither such perceptions tend;
They lose themselves in that, means to an end,
The many old producing some one new,
A last unlike the first. If lies are true,
The Caliph's wheel-work man of brass receives
A meal, munched millet grains and lettuce leaves
Together in his stomach rattle loose;
You find them perfect next day to produce:
But ne'er expect the man, on strength of that,
Can roll an iron camel-collar flat
Like Haroun's self! I tell you, what was stored
[Sidenote: And thus gets the utmost out of him.]
Bit by bit through Sordello's life, outpoured
That eve, was, for that age, a novel thing:
And round those three the People formed a ring,
Of visionary judges whose award
He recognized in full—faces that barred
Henceforth return to the old careless life,
In whose great presence, therefore, his first strife
For their sake must not be ignobly fought;
All these, for once, approved of him, he thought,
Suspended their own vengeance, chose await
The issue of this strife to reinstate
Them in the right of taking it—in fact
He must be proved king ere they could exact
Vengeance for such king's defalcation. Last,
A reason why the phrases flowed so fast
Was in his quite forgetting for a time
Himself in his amazement that the rhyme
Disguised the royalty so much: he there—
And Salinguerra yet all unaware
Who was the lord, who liegeman!

"Thus I lay
On thine my spirit and compel obey
His lord,—my liegeman,—impotent to build
Another Rome, but hardly so unskilled
In what such builder should have been, as brook
One shame beyond the charge that I forsook
His function! Free me from that shame, I bend
A brow before, suppose new years to spend,—
Allow each chance, nor fruitlessly, recur—
Measure thee with the Minstrel, then, demur
[Sidenote: He asserts the poet's rank and right,]
At any crowd he claims! That I must cede
Shamed now, my right to my especial meed—
Confess thee fitter help the world than I

Ordained its champion from eternity,
Is much: but to behold thee scorn the post
I quit in thy behalf—to hear thee boast
What makes my own despair!" And while he rung
The changes on this theme, the roof up-sprung,
The sad walls of the presence-chamber died
Into the distance, or embowering vied
With far-away Goito's vine-frontier;
And crowds of faces—(only keeping clear
The rose-light in the midst, his vantage-ground
To fight their battle from)—deep clustered round
Sordello, with good wishes no mere breath,
Kind prayers for him no vapor, since, come death,
Come life, he was fresh-sinewed every joint,
Each bone new-marrowed as whom gods anoint
Though mortal to their rescue. Now let sprawl
The snaky volumes hither! Is Typhon all
For Hercules to trample—good report
From Salinguerra only to extort?
"So was I" (closed he his inculcating,
A poet must be earth's essential king)
[Sidenote: Basing these on their proper ground,]
"So was I, royal so, and if I fail,
'T is not the royalty, ye witness quail,
But one deposed who, caring not exert
Its proper essence, trifled malapert
With accidents instead—good things assigned
As heralds of a better thing behind—
And, worthy through display of these, put forth
Never the inmost all-surpassing worth
That constitutes him king precisely since
As yet no other spirit may evince
Its like: the power he took most pride to test,
Whereby all forms of life had been professed
At pleasure, forms already on the earth,
Was but a means to power beyond, whose birth
Should, in its novelty, be kingship's proof.
Now, whether he came near or kept aloof
The several forms he longed to imitate,
Not there the kingship lay, he sees too late.
Those forms, unalterable first as last,
Proved him her copier, not the protoplast
Of nature: what would come of being free,
By action to exhibit tree for tree,
Bird, beast, for beast and bird, or prove earth bore
One veritable man or woman more?
Means to an end, such proofs are: what the end?
Let essence, whatsoe'er it be, extend—
Never contract. Already you include
The multitude; then let the multitude
Include yourself; and the result were new:

Themselves before, the multitude turn you.
This were to live and move and have, in them,
Your being, and secure a diadem
You should transmit (because no cycle yearns
Beyond itself, but on itself returns)
When, the full sphere in wane, the world o'erlaid
Long since with you, shall have in turn obeyed
Some orb still prouder, some displayer, still
More potent than the last, of human will,
[Sidenote: Recognizing true dignity in service,]
And some new king depose the old. Of such
Am I—whom pride of this elates too much?
Safe, rather say, 'mid troops of peers again;
I, with my words, hailed brother of the train
Deeds once sufficed: for, let the world roll back,
Who fails, through deeds howe'er diverse, re-track
My purpose still, my task? A teeming crust—
Air, flame, earth, wave at conflict! Then, needs must
Emerge some Calm embodied, these refer
The brawl to—yellow-bearded Jupiter?
No! Saturn; some existence like a pact
And protest against Chaos, some first fact
I' the faint of time. My deep of life, I know,
Is unavailing e'en to poorly show" ...
For here the Chief immeasurably yawned)
... "Deeds in their due gradation till Song dawned—
The fullest effluence of the finest mind,
All in degree, no way diverse in kind
From minds about it, minds which, more or less,
Lofty or low, move seeking to impress
[Sidenote: Whether successively that of epoist,]
Themselves on somewhat; but one mind has climbed
Step after step, by just ascent sublimed.
Thought is the soul of act, and, stage by stage,
Soul is from body still to disengage
As tending to a freedom which rejects
Such help and incorporeally affects
The world, producing deeds but not by deeds,
Swaying, in others, frames itself exceeds,
Assigning them the simpler tasks it used
To patiently perform till Song produced
Acts, by thoughts only, for the mind: divest
Mind of e'en Thought, and, lo, God's unexpressed
Will draws above us! All then is to win
Save that. How much for me, then? where begin
My work? About me, faces! and they flock,
The earnest faces. What shall I unlock
By song? behold me prompt, whate'er it be,
To minister: how much can mortals see
Of Life? No more than so? I take the task
And marshal you Life's elemental masque,

Show Men, on evil or on good lay stress,
[Sidenote: Dramatist, or, so to call him, analyst,]
This light, this shade make prominent, suppress
All ordinary hues that softening blend
Such natures with the level. Apprehend
Which sinner is, which saint, if I allot
Hell, Purgatory, Heaven, a blaze or blot,
To those you doubt concerning! I enwomb
Some wretched Friedrich with his red-hot tomb;
Some dubious spirit, Lombard Agilulph
With the black chastening river I engulf!
Some unapproached Matilda I enshrine
With languors of the planet of decline—
These, fail to recognize, to arbitrate
Between henceforth, to rightly estimate
Thus marshalled in the masque! Myself, the while,
As one of you, am witness, shrink or smile
At my own showing! Next age—what's to do?
The men and women stationed hitherto
Will I unstation, good and bad, conduct
Each nature to its farthest, or obstruct
At soonest, in the world: light, thwarted, breaks
A limpid purity to rainbow flakes,
Or shadow, massed, freezes to gloom: behold
How such, with fit assistance to unfold,
Or obstacles to crush them, disengage
Their forms, love, hate, hope, fear, peace make, war wage,
In presence of you all! Myself, implied
Superior now, as, by the platform's side,
I bade them do and suffer,—would last content
The world ... no—that's too far! I circumvent
A few, my masque contented, and to these
Offer unveil the last of mysteries—
Man's inmost life shall have yet freer play:
Once more I cast external things away,
And natures composite, so decompose
That" ... Why, he writes Sordello!

"How I rose,
And how have you advanced! since evermore
Yourselves effect what I was fain before
Effect, what I supplied yourselves suggest,
What I leave bare yourselves can now invest.
How we attain to talk as brothers talk,
In half-words, call things by half-names, no balk
From discontinuing old aids. To-day
Takes in account the work of Yesterday:
Has not the world a Past now, its adept
Consults ere he dispense with or accept
New aids? a single touch more may enhance,
A touch less turned to insignificance

Those structures' symmetry the past has strewed
The world with, once so bare. Leave the mere rude
[Sidenote: Who turns in due course synthetist.]
Explicit details! 't is but brother's speech,
We need, speech where an accent's change gives each
The other's soul—no speech to understand
By former audience: need was then to expand,
Expatiate—hardly were we brothers! true—
Nor I lament my small remove from you,
Nor reconstruct what stands already. Ends
Accomplished turn to means: my art intends
New structure from the ancient: as they changed
The spoils of every clime at Venice, ranged
The horned and snouted Libyan god, upright
As in his desert, by some simple bright
Clay cinerary pitcher—Thebes as Rome,
Athens as Byzant rifled, till their Dome
From earth's reputed consummations razed
A seal, the all-transmuting Triad blazed
Above. Ah, whose that fortune? Ne'ertheless
E'en he must stoop contented to express
No tithe of what's to say—the vehicle
Never sufficient: but his work is still
For faces like the faces that select
[Sidenote: This for one day: now, serve as Guelf!]
The single service I am bound effect,—
That bid me cast aside such fancies, bow
Taurello to the Guelf cause, disallow
The Kaiser's coming—which with heart, soul, strength,
I labor for, this eve, who feel at length
My past career's outrageous vanity,
And would, as it amends, die, even die
Now I first estimate the boon of life,
If death might win compliance—sure, this strife
Is right for once—the People my support."
My poor Sordello! what may we extort
By this, I wonder? Palma's lighted eyes
Turned to Taurello who, long past surprise,
Began, "You love him—what you'd say at large
Let me say briefly. First, your father's charge
To me, his friend, peruse: I guessed indeed
You were no stranger to the course decreed.
[Sidenote: Salinguerra, dislodged from his post,]
He bids me leave his children to the saints:
As for a certain project, he acquaints
The Pope with that, and offers him the best
Of your possessions to permit the rest
Go peaceably—to Ecelin, a stripe
Of soil the cursed Vicentines will gripe,
—To Alberic, a patch the Trevisan
Clutches already; extricate, who can,

Treville, Villarazzi, Puissolo,
Loria and Cartiglione!—all must go,
And with them go my hopes. 'T is lost, then! Lost
This eve, our crisis, and some pains it cost
Procuring; thirty years—as good I'd spent
Like our admonisher! But each his bent
Pursues: no question, one might live absurd
One's self this while, by deed as he by word
Persisting to obtrude an influence where
'T is made account of, much as ... nay, you fare
With twice the fortune, youngster!—I submit,
Happy to parallel my waste of wit
With the renowned Sordello's: you decide
A course for me. Romano may abide
Romano,—Bacchus! After all, what dearth
Of Ecelins and Alberies on earth?
Say there's a prize in prospect, must disgrace
Betide competitors, unless they style
Themselves Romano? Were it worth my while
To try my own luck! But an obscure place
Suits me—there wants a youth to bustle, stalk
And attitudinize—some fight, more talk,
Most flaunting badges—how, I might make clear
Since Friedrich's very purposes lie here
—Here, pity they are like to lie! For me,
With station fixed unceremoniously
Long since, small use contesting; I am but
The liegeman—you are born the lieges—shut
That gentle mouth now! or resume your kin
In your sweet self; were Palma Ecelin
For me to work with! Could that neck endure
This bauble for a cumbrous garniture,
She should ... or might one bear it for her? Stay—
I have not been so flattered many a day
As by your pale friend—Bacchus! The least help
Would lick the hind's fawn to a lion's whelp:
His neck is broad enough—a ready tongue
Beside—too writhled—but, the main thing, young—
I could ... why, look ye!"

And the badge was thrown
[Sidenote: In moving, opens a door to Sordello,]
Across Sordello's neck: This badge alone
Makes you Romano's Head—becomes superb
On your bare neck, which would, on mine, disturb
The pauldron," said Taurello. A mad act,
Nor even dreamed about before—in fact,
Not when his sportive arm rose for the nonce—
But he had dallied overmuch, this once,
With power: the thing was done, and he, aware
The thing was done, proceeded to declare—

(So like a nature made to serve, excel
In serving, only feel by service well!)
—That he would make Sordello that and more.
"As good a scheme as any. What's to pore
At in my face?" he asked—"ponder instead
This piece of news; you are Romano's Head!
One cannot slacken pace so near the goal,
Suffer my Azzo to escape heart-whole
This time! For you there's Palma to espouse—
For me, one crowning trouble ere I house
Like my compeer."

On which ensued a strange
And solemn visitation; there came change
O'er every one of them; each looked on each:
Up in the midst a truth grew, without speech.
And when the giddiness sank and the haze
Subsided, they were sitting, no amaze,
Sordello with the baldric on, his sire
[Sidenote: Who is declared Salinguerra's son,]
Silent, though his proportions seemed aspire
Momently; and, interpreting the thrill
Right at its ebb, Palma was found there still
Relating somewhat Adelaide confessed
A year ago, while dying on her breast,—
Of a contrivance that Vicenza night
When Ecelin had birth. "Their convoy's flight,
Cut off a moment, coiled inside the flame
That wallowed like a dragon at his game
The toppling city through—San Biagio rocks!
And wounded lies in her delicious locks
Retrude, the frail mother, on her face,
None of her wasted, just in one embrace
Covering her child: when, as they lifted her,
Cleaving the tumult, mighty, mightier
And mightiest Taurello's cry outbroke,
Leapt like a tongue of fire that cleaves the smoke,
Midmost to cheer his Mantuans onward—drown
His colleague Ecelin's clamor, up and down
The disarray: failed Adelaide see then
Who was the natural chief, the man of men?
Outstripping time, her infant there burst swathe,
Stood up with eyes haggard beyond the scathe
From wandering after his heritage
Lost once and lost for aye—and why that rage,
That deprecating glance? A new shape leant
On a familiar shape—gloatingly bent
O'er his discomfiture; 'mid wreaths it wore,
Still one outflamed the rest—her child's before
'T was Salinguerra's for his child: scorn, hate,
Rage now might startle her when all too late!

Then was the moment!—rival's foot had spurned

[Sidenote: Hidden hitherto by Adelaide's policy.]

Never that House to earth else! Sense returned—
The act conceived, adventured and complete,
They bore away to an obscure retreat
Mother and child—Retrude's self not slain"
(Nor even here Taurello moved) "though pain
Was fled: and what assured them most 't was fled,
All pain, was, if they raised the pale hushed head
'T would turn this way and that, waver awhile,
And only settle into its old smile—
(Graceful as the disquieted water-flag
Steadying itself, remarked they, in the quag
On either side their path)—when suffered look
Down on her child. They marched: no sign once shook
The company's close litter of crossed spears
Till, as they reached Goito, a few tears
Slipped in the sunset from her long black lash,
And she was gone. So far the action rash;
No crime. They laid Retrude in the font,
Taurello's very gift, her child was wont
To sit beneath—constant as eve he came
To sit by its attendant girls the same
As one of them. For Palma, she would blend
With this magnific spirit to the end,
That ruled her first; but scarcely had she dared
To disobey the Adelaide who scared
Her into vowing never to disclose
A secret to her husband, which so froze
His blood at half-recital, she contrived
To hide from him Taurello's infant lived,
Lest, by revealing that, himself should mar
Romano's fortunes. And, a crime so far,
Palma received that action: she was told
Of Salinguerra's nature, of his cold
Calm acquiescence in his lot! But free
To impart the secret to Romano, she

[Sidenote: How the discovery moves Salinguerra,]

Engaged to repossess Sordello of
His heritage, and hers, and that way doff
The mask, but after years, long years: while now,
Was not Romano's sign-mark on that brow?"
Across Taurello's heart his arms were locked:
And when he did speak 'twas as if he mocked
The minstrel, "who had not to move," he said,
"Nor stir—should fate defraud him of a shred
Of his son's infancy? much less his youth!"
(Laughingly all this)—"which to aid, in truth,
Himself, reserved on purpose, had not grown
Old, not too old—'twas best they kept alone
Till now, and never idly met till now;"

—Then, in the same breath, told Sordello how
All intimations of this eve's event
Were lies, for Friedrich must advance to Trent,
Thence to Verona, then to Rome, there stop,
Tumble the Church down, institute a-top
The Alps a Prefecture of Lombardy:
—"That's now!—no prophesying what may be
Anon, with a new monarch of the clime,
Native of Gesi, passing his youth's prime
At Naples. Tito bids my choice decide
On whom" ...

"Embrace him, madman!" Palma cried,
Who through the laugh saw sweat-drops burst apace,
And his lips blanching: he did not embrace
Sordello, but he laid Sordello's hand
On his own eyes, mouth, forehead.

Understand,
This while Sordello was becoming flushed
[Sidenote: And Sordello the finally-determined,]
Out of his whiteness; thoughts rushed, fancies rushed;
He pressed his hand upon his head and signed
Both should forbear him. "Nay, the best's behind!"
Taurello laughed—not quite with the same laugh:
"The truth is, thus we scatter, ay, like chaff
These Guelfs, a despicable monk recoils
From: nor expect a fickle Kaiser spoils
Our triumph!—Friedrich? Think you, I intend
Friedrich shall reap the fruits of blood I spend
And brain I waste? Think you, the people clap
Their hands at my out-hewing this wild gap
For any Friedrich to fill up? 'Tis mine—
That's yours: I tell you, towards some such design
Have I worked blindly, yes, and idly, yes,
And for another, yes—but worked no less
With instinct at my heart; I else had swerved,
While now—look round! My cunning has preserved
Samminiato—that's a central place
Secures us Florence, boy,—in Pisa's case,
By land as she by sea; with Pisa ours,
And Florence, and Pistoia, one devours
The land at leisure! Gloriously dispersed—
Brescia, observe, Milan, Piacenza first
That flanked us (ah, you know not!) in the March;
On these we pile, as keystone of our arch,
Romagna and Bologna, whose first span
Covered the Trentine and the Valsugan;
Sofia's Egna by Bolgiano's sure!" ...
So he proceeded: half of all this, pure
[Sidenote: The devil putting forth his potency:]

Delusion, doubtless, nor the rest too true,
But what was undone he felt sure to do,
As ring by ring he wrung off, flung away
The pauldron-rings to give his sword-arm play—
Need of the sword now! That would soon adjust
Aught wrong at present; to the sword intrust
Sordello's whiteness, undersize: 'twas plain
He hardly rendered right to his own brain—
Like a brave hound, men educate to pride
Himself on speed or scent nor aught beside,
As though he could not, gift by gift, match men!
[Sidenote: Since Sordello, who began by rhyming,]
Palma had listened patiently: but when
'Twas time expostulate, attempt withdraw
Taurello from his child, she, without awe
Took off his iron arms from, one by one,
Sordello's shrinking shoulders, and, that done,
Made him avert his visage and relieve
Sordello (you might see his corselet heave
The while) who, loose, rose—tried to speak, then sank:
They left him in the chamber. All was blank.
And even reeling down the narrow stair
Taurello kept up, as though unaware
Palma was by to guide him, the old device
—Something of Milan—"how we muster thrice
The Torriani's strength there; all along
Our own Visconti cowed them"—thus the song
Continued even while she bade him stoop,
Thrid somehow, by some glimpse of arrow-loop,
The turnings to the gallery below,
Where he stopped short as Palma let him go.
When he had sat in silence long enough
Splintering the stone bench, braving a rebuff
She stopped the truncheon; only to commence
One of Sordello's poems, a pretence
For speaking, some poor rhyme of "Elys' hair
And head that's sharp and perfect like a pear,
So smooth and close are laid the few fine locks
[Sidenote: May, even from the depths of failure]
Stained like pale honey oozed from topmost rocks
Sun-blanched the livelong summer"—from his worst
Performance, the Goito, as his first:
And that at end, conceiving from the brow
And open mouth no silence would serve now,
Went on to say the whole world loved that man
And, for that matter, thought his face, though wan,
Eclipsed the Count's—he sucking in each phrase
As if an angel spoke. The foolish praise
Ended, he drew her on his mailed knees, made
Her face a framework with his hands, a shade,
A crown, an aureole: there must she remain

(Her little mouth compressed with smiling pain
As in his gloves she felt her tresses twitch)
To get the best look at, in fittest niche
Dispose his saint. That done, he kissed her brow,
—"Lauded her father for his treason now,"
He told her, "only, how could one suspect
The wit in him?—whose clansman, recollect,
Was ever Salinguerra—she, the same,
Romano and his lady—so, might claim
To know all, as she should"—and thus begun
Schemes with a vengeance, schemes on schemes, "not one
Fit to be told that foolish boy," he said,
"But only let Sordello Palma wed,
—Then!"

'T was a dim long narrow place at best:
[Sidenote: Yet spring to the summit of success,]
Midway a sole grate showed the fiery West,
As shows its corpse the world's end some split tomb—
A gloom, a rift of fire, another gloom,
Faced Palma—but at length Taurello set
Her free; the grating held one ragged jet
Of fierce gold fire: he lifted her within
The hollow underneath—how else begin
Fate's second marvellous cycle, else renew
The ages than with Palma plain in view?
Then paced the passage, hands clenched, head erect,
Pursuing his discourse; a grand unchecked
Monotony made out from his quick talk
And the recurring noises of his walk;
—Somewhat too much like the o'ercharged assent
Of two resolved friends in one danger blent,
Who hearten each the other against heart;
Boasting there 's naught to care for, when, apart
The boaster, all 's to care for. He, beside
Some shape not visible, in power and pride
Approached, out of the dark, ginglingly near,
Nearer, passed close in the broad light, his ear
Crimson, eyeballs suffused, temples full-fraught,
Just a snatch of the rapid speech you caught,
And on he strode into the opposite dark,
Till presently the harsh heel's turn, a spark
I' the stone, and whirl of some loose embossed thong
That crashed against the angle aye so long
After the last, punctual to an amount
Of mailed great paces you could not but count,—
Prepared you for the pacing back again.
And by the snatches you might ascertain
That, Friedrich's Prefecture surmounted, left
By this alone in Italy, they cleft
Asunder, crushed together, at command

Of none, were free to break up Hildebrand,
[Sidenote: If he consent to oppress the world.]
Rebuild, he and Sordello, Charlemagne—
But garnished, Strength with Knowledge, "if we deign
Accept that compromise and stoop to give
Rome law, the Cæsar's Representative."
Enough, that the illimitable flood
Of triumphs after triumphs, understood
In its faint reflux (you shall hear) sufficed
Young Ecelin for appanage, enticed
Him on till, these long quiet in their graves,
He found 't was looked for that a whole life's braves
Should somehow be made good; so, weak and worn,
Must stagger up at Milan, one gray morn
Of the to-come, and fight his latest fight.
But, Salinguerra's prophecy at height—
[Sidenote: Just this decided, as it now may be,]
He voluble with a raised arm and stiff,
A blaring voice, a blazing eye, as if
He had our very Italy to keep
Or cast away, or gather in a heap
To garrison the better—ay, his word
Was, "run the cucumber into a gourd,
Drive Trent upon Apulia"—at their pitch
Who spied the continents and islands which
Grew mulberry-leaves and sickles, in the map—
(Strange that three such confessions so should hap
To Palma, Dante spoke with in the clear
Amorous silence of the Swooning-sphere,—
Cunizza, as he called her! Never ask
Of Palma more! She sat, knowing her task
Was done, the labor of it,—for, success
Concerned not Palma, passion's votaress)
Triumph at height, and thus Sordello crowned—
Above the passage suddenly a sound
Stops speech, stops walk: back shrinks Taurello, bids
With large involuntary asking lids,
Palma interpret. "'T is his own foot-stamp—
Your hand! His summons! Nay, this idle damp
Befits not!" Out they two reeled dizzily.
"Visconti 's strong at Milan," resumed he,
In the old, somewhat insignificant way—
(Was Palma wont, years afterward, to say)
As though the spirit's flight, sustained thus far,
Dropped at that very instant.

Gone they are—
Palma, Taurello; Eglamor anon,
Ecelin,—only Naddo 's never gone!
—Labors, this moonrise, what the Master meant—
"Is Squarcialupo speckled?—purulent,

I 'd say, but when was Providence put out?
He carries somehow handily about
His spite nor fouls himself!" Goito's vines
Stand like a cheat detected—stark rough lines,
The moon breaks through, a gray mean scale against
The vault where, this eve's Maiden, thou remain'st
Like some fresh martyr, eyes fixed—who can tell?
As Heaven, now all 's at end, did not so well,
[Sidenote: And we have done.]
Spite of the faith and victory, to leave
Its virgin quite to death in the lone eve.
While the persisting hermit-bee ... ha! wait
No longer: these in compass, forward fate!

BOOK THE SIXTH

The thought of Eglamor's least like a thought,
[Sidenote: At the close of a day or a life,]
And yet a false one, was, "Man shrinks to naught
If matched with symbols of immensity;
Must quail, forsooth, before a quiet sky
Or sea, too little for their quietude:"
And, truly, somewhat in Sordello's mood
Confirmed its speciousness, while eve slow sank
Down the near terrace to the farther bank,
And only one spot left from out the night
Glimmered, upon the river opposite—
A breadth of watery heaven like a bay,
A sky-like space of water, ray for ray,
And star for star, one richness where they mixed
As this and that wing of an angel, fixed,
Tumultuary splendors folded in
To die. Nor turned he till Ferrara's din
(Say, the monotonous speech from a man's lip
Who lets some first and eager purpose slip
In a new fancy's birth; the speech keeps on
Though elsewhere its informing soul be gone)
—Aroused him, surely offered succor. Fate
Paused with this eve; ere she precipitate
Herself,—best put off new strange thoughts awhile,
That voice, those large hands, that portentous smile,—
What help to pierce the future as the past,
Lay in the plaining city?

And at last
The main discovery and prime concern,
All that just now imported him to learn,
Truth's self, like yonder slow moon to complete
Heaven, rose again, and, naked at his feet,

Lighted his old life's every shift and change,
[Sidenote: Past procedure is fitliest reviewed,]
Effort with counter-effort; nor the range
Of each looked wrong except wherein it checked
Some other—which of these could he suspect,
Prying into them by the sudden blaze?
The real way seemed made up of all the ways—
Mood after mood of the one mind in him;
Tokens of the existence, bright or dim,
Of a transcendent all-embracing sense
Demanding only outward influence,
A soul, in Palma's phrase, above his soul,
Power to uplift his power,—such moon's control
Over such sea-depths,—and their mass had swept
Onward from the beginning and still kept
Its course: but years and years the sky above
Held none, and so, untasked of any love,
His sensitiveness idled, now amort,
Alive now, and, to sullenness or sport
Given wholly up, disposed itself anew
At every passing instigation, grew
And dwindled at caprice, in foam-showers spilt,
Wedge-like insisting, quivered now a gilt
Shield in the sunshine, now a blinding race
Of whitest ripples o'er the reef—found place
For much display; not gathered up and, hurled
Right from its heart, encompassing the world.
So had Sordello been, by consequence,
Without a function: others made pretence
To strength not half his own, yet had some core
Within, submitted to some moon, before
Them still, superior still whate'er their force,—
Were able therefore to fulfil a course,
Nor missed life's crown, authentic attribute.
To each who lives must be a certain fruit
Of having lived in his degree,—a stage,
Earlier or later in men's pilgrimage,
To stop at; and to this the spirits tend
Who, still discovering beauty without end,
Amass the scintillations, make one star
—Something unlike them, self-sustained, afar,—
And meanwhile nurse the dream of being blest
By winning it to notice and invest
Their souls with alien glory, some one day
[Sidenote: As more appreciable in its entirety.]
Whene'er the nucleus, gathering shape alway,
Round to the perfect circle—soon or late;
According as themselves are formed to wait;
Whether mere human beauty will suffice
—The yellow hair and the luxurious eyes,
Or human intellect seem best, or each

Combine in some ideal form past reach
On earth, or else some shade of these, some aim,
Some love, hate even, take their place, the same,
So to be served—all this they do not lose,
Waiting for death to live, nor idly choose
What must be Hell—a progress thus pursued
Through all existence, still above the food
That 's offered them; still fain to reach beyond
The widened range, in virtue of their bond
Of sovereignty. Not that a Palma's Love,
A Salinguerra's Hate, would equal prove
To swaying all Sordello: but why doubt
[Sidenote: Strong, he needed external strength:]
Some love meet for such strength, some moon without
Would match his sea?—or fear, Good manifest,
Only the Best breaks faith?—Ah, but the Best
Somehow eludes us ever, still might be
And is not! Crave we gems? No penury
Of their material round us! Pliant earth
And plastic flame—what balks the mage his birth
—Jacinth in balls or lodestone by the block?
Flinders enrich the strand, veins swell the rock;
Naught more! Seek creatures? Life 's i' the tempest, thought
Clothes the keen hill-top, mid-day woods are fraught
With fervors: human forms are well enough!
But we had hoped, encouraged by the stuff
Profuse at nature's pleasure, men beyond
These actual men!—and thus are over-fond
In arguing, from Good—the Best, from force
Divided—force combined, an ocean's course
From this our sea whose mere intestine pants
Might seem at times sufficient to our wants.

External power? If none be adequate,
And he stand forth ordained (a prouder fate)
Himself a law to his own sphere?—remove
All incompleteness, for that law, that love?
Nay, if all other laws be feints,—truth veiled
Helpfully to weak vision that had failed
To grasp aught but its special want,—for lure,
Embodied? Stronger vision could endure
The unbodied want: no part—the whole of truth!
The People were himself; nor, by the ruth
At their condition, was he less impelled
[Sidenote: Even now, where can he perceive such?]
To alter the discrepancy beheld,
Than if, from the sound whole, a sickly part
Subtracted were transformed, decked out with art,
Then palmed on him as alien woe—the Guelf
To succor, proud that he forsook himself.
[Sidenote: Internal strength must suffice then,]

All is himself; all service, therefore, rates
Alike, nor serving one part, immolates
The rest: but all in time! "That lance of yours
Makes havoc soon with Malek and his Moors,
That buckler's lined with many a giant's beard,
Ere long, our champion, be the lance upreared,
The buckler wielded handsomely as now!
But view your escort, bear in mind your vow,
Count the pale tracts of sand to pass ere that,
And, if you hope we struggle through the flat,
Put lance and buckler by! Next half-month lacks
Mere sturdy exercise of mace and axe
To cleave this dismal brake of prickly-pear
Which bristling holds Cydippe by the hair,
Lames barefoot Agathon: this felled, we'll try
The picturesque achievements by and by—
Next life!"

Ay, rally, mock, O People, urge
Your claims!—for thus he ventured, to the verge,
Push a vain mummery which perchance distrust
Of his fast-slipping resolution thrust
Likewise: accordingly the Crowd—(as yet
He had unconsciously contrived forget,
I' the whole, to dwell o' the points ... one might assuage
The signal horrors easier than engage
With a dim vulgar vast unobvious grief
Not to be fancied off, nor gained relief
In brilliant fits, cured by a happy quirk,
But by dim vulgar vast unobvious work
To corrrespond ...)—this Crowd then, forth they stood.
"And now content thy stronger vision, brood
On thy bare want; uncovered, turf by turf,
Study the corpse-face through the taint-worms' scurf!"

Down sank the People's Then; up-rose their Now
These sad ones render service to! And how
[Sidenote: His sympathy with the people, to wit;]
Piteously little must that service prove
—Had surely proved in any case! for, move
Each other obstacle away, let youth
Become aware it had surprised a truth
'T were service to impart—can truth be seized,
Settled forthwith, and, of the captive eased,
Its captor find fresh prey, since this alit
So happily, no gesture luring it,
The earnest of a flock to follow? Vain,
Most vain! a life to spend ere this he chain
To the poor crowd's complacence: ere the crowd
Pronounce it captured, he descries a cloud
Its kin of twice the plume; which he, in turn,

If he shall live as many lives, may learn
How to secure: not else. Then Mantua called
Back to his mind how certain bards were thralled
—Buds blasted, but of breath more like perfume
Than Naddo's staring nosegay's carrion bloom;
Some insane rose that burnt heart out in sweets,
A spendthrift in the spring, no summer greets;
Some Dularete, drunk with truths and wine,
Grown bestial, dreaming how become divine.
Yet to surmount this obstacle, commence
With the commencement, merits crowning! Hence
Must truth be casual truth, elicited
In sparks so mean, at intervals dispread
So rarely, that 'tis like at no one time
Of the world's story has not truth, the prime
Of truth, the very truth which, loosed, had hurled
The world's course right, been really in the world
—Content the while with some mean spark by dint
Of some chance-blow, the solitary hint
Of buried fire, which, rip earth's breast, would stream
Sky-ward!

Sordello's miserable gleam
Was looked for at the moment: he would dash
This badge, and all it brought, to earth,—abash
Taurello thus, perhaps persuade him wrest
The Kaiser from his purpose,—would attest
His own belief, in any case. Before
[Sidenote: Of which, try now the inherent force!]
He dashes it however, think once more!
For, were that little, truly service? "Ay,
I' the end, no doubt; but meantime? Plain you spy
Its ultimate effect, but many flaws
Of vision blur each intervening cause.
Were the day's fraction clear as the life's sum
Of service, Now as filled as teems To-come
With evidence of good—nor too minute
A share to vie with evil! No dispute,
'Twere fitliest maintain the Guelfs in rule:
That makes your life's work: but you have to school
Your day's work on these natures circumstanced
Thus variously, which yet, as each advanced
Or might impede the Guelf rule, must be moved
Now, for the Then's sake,—hating what you loved,
Loving old hatreds! Nor if one man bore
Brand upon temples while his fellow wore
The aureole, would it task you to decide:
But, portioned duly out, the future vied
Never with the unparcelled present! Smite
Or spare so much on warrant all so slight?
The present's complete sympathies to break,

Aversions bear with, for a future's sake
So feeble? Tito ruined through one speck.
The Legate saved by his sole lightish fleck?
This were work, true, but work performed at cost
Of other work; aught gained here, elsewhere lost.
For a new segment spoil an orb half-done?
Rise with the People one step, and sink—one?
Were it but one step, less than the whole face
Of things, your novel duty bids erase!
Harms to abolish! What, the prophet saith,
The minstrel singeth vainly then? Old faith,
Old courage, only born because of harms,
Were not, from highest to the lowest, charms?
Flame may persist; but is not glare as stanch?
Where the salt marshes stagnate, crystals branch;
Blood dries to crimson; Evil's beautified
In every shape. Thrust Beauty then aside
And banish Evil! Wherefore? After all,
Is Evil a result less natural
Than Good? For overlook the seasons' strife
With tree and flower,—the hideous animal life,
(Of which who seeks shall find a grinning taunt
[Sidenote: How much of man's ill may be removed?]
For his solution, and endure the vaunt
Of nature's angel, as a child that knows
Himself befooled, unable to propose
Aught better than the fooling)—and but care
For men, for the mere People then and there,—
In these, could you but see that Good and Ill
Claimed you alike! Whence rose their claim but still
From Ill, as fruit of Ill? What else could knit
You theirs but Sorrow? Any free from it
Were also free from you! Whose happiness
Could be distinguished in this morning's press
Of miseries?—the fool's who passed a gibe
'On thee,' jeered he, so wedded to thy tribe,
Thou carriest green and yellow tokens in
Thy very face that thou art Ghibellin!'
Much hold on you that fool obtained! Nay mount
Yet higher—and upon men's own account
[Sidenote: How much of ill ought to be removed?]
Must evil stay: for, what is joy?—to heave
Up one obstruction more, and common leave
What was peculiar, by such act destroy
Itself; a partial death is every joy;
The sensible escape, enfranchisement
Of a sphere's essence: once the vexed—content,
The cramped—at large, the growing circle—round,
All's to begin again—some novel bound
To break, some new enlargement to entreat;
The sphere though larger is not more complete.

Now for Mankind's experience: who alone
Might style the unobstructed world his own?
Whom palled Goito with its perfect things?
Sordello's self: whereas for Mankind springs
Salvation by each hindrance interposed.
They climb; life's view is not at once disclosed
To creatures caught up, on the summit left,
Heaven plain above them, yet of wings bereft:
But lower laid, as at the mountain's foot.
So, range on range, the girdling forests shoot
Twixt your plain prospect and the throngs who scale
Height after height, and pierce mists, veil by veil,
Heartened with each discovery; in their soul,
The Whole they seek by Parts—but, found that Whole,
Could they revert, enjoy past gains? The space
Of time you judge so meagre to embrace
The Parts were more than plenty, once attained
The Whole, to quite exhaust it: naught were gained
But leave to look—not leave to do: Beneath
Soon sates the looker—look above, and Death
Tempts ere a tithe of Life be tasted. Live
First, and die soon enough, Sordello! Give
[Sidenote: If removed, at what cost to Sordello?]
Body and spirit the first right they claim,
And pasture soul on a voluptuous shame
That you, a pageant-city's denizen,
Are neither vilely lodged 'midst Lombard men—
Can force joy out of sorrow, seem to truck
Bright attributes away for sordid muck,
Yet manage from that very muck educe
Gold; then subject nor scruple, to your cruce
The world's discardings! Though real ingots pay
Your pains, the clods that yielded them are clay
To all beside,—would clay remain, though quenched
Your purging-fire; who's robbed then? Had you wrenched
An ampler treasure forth!—As 't is, they crave
A share that ruins you and will not save
Them. Why should sympathy command you quit
The course that makes your joy, nor will remit
Their woe? Would all arrive at joy? Reverse
[Sidenote: Men win little thereby; he loses all:]
The order (time instructs you) nor coerce
Each unit till, some predetermined mode,
The total be emancipate; men's road
Is one, men's times of travel many; thwart
No enterprising soul's precocious start
Before the general march! If slow or fast
All straggle up to the same point at last,
Why grudge your having gained, a month ago,
The brakes at balm-shed, asphodels in blow,
While they were landlocked? Speed their Then, but how

This badge would suffer you improve your Now!"
His time of action for, against, or with
Our world (I labor to extract the pith
Of this his problem) grew, that even-tide,
Gigantic with its power of joy, beside
The world's eternity of impotence
To profit though at his whole joy's expense.
[Sidenote: For he can infinitely enjoy himself,]
"Make nothing of my day because so brief?
Rather make more: instead of joy, use grief
Before its novelty have time subside!
Wait not for the late savor, leave untried
Virtue, the creaming honey-wine, quick squeeze
Vice like a biting spirit from the lees
Of life! Together let wrath, hatred, lust,
All tyrannies in every shape, be thrust
Upon this Now, which time may reason out
As mischiefs, far from benefits, no doubt;
But long ere then Sordello will have slipped
Away; you teach him at Goito's crypt,
There 's a blank issue to that fiery thrill.
Stirring, the few cope with the many, still:
So much of sand as, quiet, makes a mass
Unable to produce three tufts of grass,
Shall, troubled by the whirlwind, render void
The whole calm glebe's endeavor: he employed!
And e'en though somewhat smart the Crowd for this,
Contribute each his pang to make your bliss,
'T is but one pang—one blood-drop to the bowl
Which brimful tempts the sluggish asp uncowl
At last, stains ruddily the dull red cape,
And, kindling orbs gray as the unripe grape
Before, avails forthwith to disentrance
The portent, soon to lead a mystic dance
Among you! For, who sits alone in Rome?
Have those great hands indeed hewn out a home,
And set me there to live? Oh life, life-breath,
Life-blood,—ere sleep, come travail, life ere death!
This life stream on my soul, direct, oblique,
But always streaming! Hindrances? They pique:
Helps? such ... but why repeat, my soul o'er-tops
Each height, then every depth profoundlier drops?
Enough that I can live, and would live! Wait
For some transcendent life reserved by Fate
To follow this? Oh, never! Fate, I trust
The same, my soul to; for, as who flings dust,
Perchance (so facile was the deed) she checked
The void with these materials to affect
My soul diversely: these consigned anew
To naught by death, what marvel if she threw
A second and superber spectacle

Before me? What may serve for sun, what still
Wander a moon above me? What else wind
About me like the pleasures left behind,
And how shall some new flesh that is not flesh
Cling to me? What 's new laughter? Soothes the fresh
Sleep like sleep? Fate 's exhaustless for my sake
In brave resource: but whether bids she slake
My thirst at this first rivulet, or count
No draught worth lip save from some rocky fount
Above i' the clouds, while here she 's provident
Of pure loquacious pearl, the soft tree-tent
Guards, with its face of reate and sedge, nor fail
The silver globules and gold-sparkling grail
At bottom? Oh, 't were too absurd to slight
For the hereafter the to-day's delight!
Quench thirst at this, then seek next well-spring: wear
Home-lilies ere strange lotus in my hair!
Here is the Crowd, whom I with freest heart
Offer to serve, contented for my part
[Sidenote: Freed from a problematic obligation,]
To give life up in service,—only grant
That I do serve; if otherwise, why want
Aught further of me? If men cannot choose
But set aside life, why should I refuse
The gift? I take it—I, for one, engage
Never to falter through my pilgrimage—
Nor end it howling that the stock or stone
Were enviable, truly: I, for one,
Will praise the world, you style mere anteroom
To palace—be it so! shall I assume
—My foot the courtly gait, my tongue the trope,
My mouth the smirk, before the doors fly ope
One moment? What? with guarders row on row,
Gay swarms of varletry that come and go,
Pages to dice with, waiting-girls unlace
The plackets of, pert claimants help displace,
Heart-heavy suitors get a rank for,—laugh
At yon sleek parasite, break his own staff
'Cross Beetle-brows the Usher's shoulder,—why,
Admitted to the presence by and by,
Should thought of having lost these make me grieve
Among new joys I reach, for joys I leave?
Cool citrine-crystals, fierce pyropus-stone,
Are floor-work there! But do I let alone
That black-eyed peasant in the vestibule
Once and forever?—Floor-work? No such fool!
Rather, were heaven to forestall earth, I'd say
I, is it, must be blessed? Then, my own way
[Sidenote: And accepting life on its own terms,]
Bless me! Give firmer arm and fleeter foot,
I 'll thank you: but to no mad wings transmute

These limbs of mine—our greensward was so soft!
Nor camp I on the thunder-cloud aloft:
We feel the bliss distinctlier, having thus
Engines subservient, not mixed up with us.
Better move palpably through heaven: nor, freed
Of flesh, forsooth, from space to space proceed
'Mid flying synods of worlds! No: in heaven's marge
Show Titan still, recumbent o'er his targe
Solid with stars—the Centaur at his game,
Made tremulously out in hoary flame!
"Life! Yet the very cup whose extreme dull
Dregs, even, I would quaff, was dashed, at full,
Aside so oft; the death I fly, revealed
So oft a better life this life concealed,
And which sage, champion, martyr, through each path
[Sidenote: Which, yet, others have renounced: how?]
Have hunted fearlessly—the horrid bath,
The crippling-irons and the fiery chair.
'T was well for them; let me become aware
As they, and I relinquish life, too! Let
What masters life disclose itself! Forget
Vain ordinances, I have one appeal—
I feel, am what I feel, know what I feel;
So much is truth to me. What Is, then? Since
One object, viewed diversely, may evince
Beauty and ugliness—this way attract,
That way repel,—why gloze upon the fact?
Why must a single of the sides be right?
What bids choose this and leave the opposite?
Where's abstract Right for me?—in youth endued
With Right still present, still to be pursued,
Through all the interchange of circles, rife
Each with its proper law and mode of life,
Each to be dwelt at ease in: where, to sway
Absolute with the Kaiser, or obey
Implicit with his serf of fluttering heart,
Or, like a sudden thought of God's, to start
Up, Brutus in the presence, then go shout
That some should pick the unstrung jewels out—
Each, well!"

And, as in moments when the past
Gave partially enfranchisement, he cast
Himself quite through mere secondary states
Of his soul's essence, little loves and hates,
[Sidenote: Because there is a life beyond life,]
Into the mid deep yearnings overlaid
By these; as who should pierce hill, plain, grove, glade,
And on into the very nucleus probe
That first determined there exist a globe.
As that were easiest, half the globe dissolved,

So seemed Sordello's closing-truth evolved
By his flesh-half's break up; the sudden swell
Of his expanding soul showed Ill and Well,
Sorrow and Joy, Beauty and Ugliness,
Virtue and Vice, the Larger and the Less,
All qualities, in fine, recorded here,
Might be but modes of Time and this one sphere,
Urgent on these, but not of force to bind
Eternity, as Time—as Matter—Mind,
If Mind, Eternity, should choose assert
Their attributes within a Life: thus girt
With circumstance, next change beholds them cinct
Quite otherwise—with Good and Ill distinct,
Joys, sorrows, tending to a like result—
Contrived to render easy, difficult,
This or the other course of ... what new bond
In place of flesh may stop their flight beyond
Its new sphere, as that course does harm or good
To its arrangements. Once this understood,
As suddenly he felt himself alone,
Quite out of Time and this world: all was known.
What made the secret of his past despair?
—Most imminent when he seemed most aware
Of his own self-sufficiency; made mad
By craving to expand the power he had,
And not new power to be expanded?—just
This made it; Soul on Matter being thrust,
Joy comes when so much Soul is wreaked in Time
On Matter,—let the Soul's attempt sublime
Matter beyond the scheme and so prevent
By more or less that deed's accomplishment,
And Sorrow follows: Sorrow how avoid?
Let the employer match the thing employed,
Fit to the finite his infinity.
And thus proceed forever, in degree
[Sidenote: And with new conditions of success,]
Changed but in kind the same, still limited
To the appointed circumstance and dead
To all beyond. A sphere is but a sphere;
Small, Great, are merely terms we bandy here;
Since to the spirit's absoluteness all
Are like. Now, of the present sphere we call
Life, are conditions; take but this among
Many; the body was to be so long
Youthful, no longer: but, since no control
Tied to that body's purposes his soul,
She chose to understand the body's trade
More than the body's self—had fain conveyed
Her boundless, to the body's bounded lot.
Hence, the soul permanent, the body not,—
Scarcely its minute for enjoying here,—

The soul must needs instruct her weak compeer,
Run o'er its capabilities and wring
A joy thence, she held worth experiencing:
Which, far from half discovered even,—lo,
The minute gone, the body's power let go
Apportioned to that joy's acquirement! Broke
[Sidenote: Nor such as, in this, produce failure.]
Morning o'er earth, he yearned for all it woke—
From the volcano's vapor-flag, winds hoist
Black o'er the spread of sea,—down to the moist
Dale's silken barley-spikes sullied with rain,
Swayed earthwards, heavily to rise again—
The Small, a sphere as perfect as the Great
To the soul's absoluteness. Meditate
Too long on such a morning's cluster-chord
And the whole music it was framed afford,—
The chord's might half discovered, what should pluck
One string, his finger, was found palsy-struck.
And then no marvel if the spirit, shown
A saddest sight—the body lost alone
Through her officious proffered help, deprived
Of this and that enjoyment Fate contrived,—
Virtue, Good, Beauty, each allowed slip hence,—
Vaingloriously were fain, for recompense,
To stem the ruin even yet, protract
The body's term, supply the power it lacked
From her infinity, compel it learn
These qualities were only Time's concern,
And body may, with spirit helping, barred—
Advance the same, vanquished—obtain reward,
Reap joy where sorrow was intended grow,
Of Wrong make Right, and turn Ill Good below.
And the result is, the poor body soon
Sinks under what was meant a wondrous boon,
Leaving its bright accomplice all aghast.
So much was plain then, proper in the past;
To be complete for, satisfy the whole
Series of spheres—Eternity, his soul
Needs must exceed, prove incomplete for, each
Single sphere—Time. But does our knowledge reach
No farther? Is the cloud of hindrance broke
[Sidenote: But, even here, is failure inevitable?]
But by the failing of the fleshly yoke,
Its loves and hates, as now when death lets soar
Sordello, self-sufficient as before,
Though during the mere space that shall elapse
'Twixt his enthralment in new bonds, perhaps?
Must life be ever just escaped, which should
Have been enjoyed?—nay, might have been and would,
Each purpose ordered right—the soul's no whit
Beyond the body's purpose under it—

Like yonder breadth of watery heaven, a bay,
And that sky-space of water, ray for ray
And star for star, one richness where they mixed
As this and that wing of an angel, fixed,
Tumultuary splendors folded in
To die—would soul, proportioned thus, begin
Exciting discontent, or surelier quell
The body if, aspiring, it rebel?
But how so order life? Still brutalize
The soul, the sad world's way, with muffled eyes
To all that was before, all that shall be
After this sphere—all and each quality
Save some sole and immutable Great-Good
And Beauteous whither fate has loosed its hood
[Sidenote: Or may failure here be success also]
To follow? Never may some soul see All
—The Great Before and After, and the Small
Now, yet be saved by this the simplest lore,
And take the single course prescribed before,
As the king-bird with ages on his plumes
Travels to die in his ancestral glooms?
But where descry the Love that shall select
That course? Here is a soul whom, to affect,
Nature has plied with all her means, from trees
And flowers e'en to the Multitude!—and these,
Decides he save or no? One word to end!
Ah, my Sordello, I this once befriend
And speak for you. Of a Power above you still
Which, utterly incomprehensible,
Is out of rivalry, which thus you can
[Sidenote: When induced by love?]
Love, though unloving all conceived by man—
What need! And of—none the minutest duct
To that out-nature, naught that would instruct
And so let rivalry begin to live—
But of a Power its representative
Who, being for authority the same,
Communication different, should claim
A course, the first chose but this last revealed—
This Human clear, as that Divine concealed—
What utter need!

What has Sordello found?
Or can his spirit go the mighty round,
End where poor Eglamor begun? So, says
Old fable, the two eagles went two ways
About the world: where, in the midst, they met,
Though on a shifting waste of sand, men set
Jove's temple. Quick, what has Sordello found?
[Sidenote: Sordello knows:]
For they approach—approach—that foot's rebound

Palma? No, Salinguerra though in mail;
They mount, have reached the threshold, dash the veil
Aside—and you divine who sat there dead,
Under his foot the badge: still, Palma said,
A triumph lingering in the wide eyes,
Wider than some spent swimmer's if he spies
Help from above in his extreme despair,
And, head far back on shoulder thrust, turns there
With short quick passionate cry: as Palma pressed
In one great kiss, her lips upon his breast,
It beat.

By this, the hermit-bee has stopped
His day's toil at Goito: the new-cropped
Dead vine-leaf answers, now 't is eve, he bit,
Twirled so, and filed all day: the mansion's fit,
God counselled for. As easy guess the word
That passed betwixt them, and become the third
To the soft small unfrighted bee, as tax
Him with one fault—so, no remembrance racks
[Sidenote: But too late: an insect knows sooner.]
Of the stone maidens and the font of stone
He, creeping through the crevice, leaves alone.
Alas, my friend, alas Sordello, whom
Anon they laid within that old font-tomb,
And, yet again, alas!

And now is 't worth
Our while bring back to mind, much less set forth
How Salinguerra extricates himself
Without Sordello? Ghibellin and Guelf
May fight their fiercest out? If Richard sulked
In durance or the Marquis paid his mulct,
Who cares, Sordello gone? The upshot, sure,
[Sidenote: On his disappearance from the stage,]
Was peace; our chief made some frank overture
That prospered; compliment fell thick and fast
On its disposer, and Taurello passed
With foe and friend for an outstripping soul,
Nine days at least. Then,—fairly reached the goal,—
He, by one effort, blotted the great hope
Out of his mind, nor further tried to cope
With Este, that mad evening's style, but sent
Away the Legate and the League, content
No blame at least the brothers had incurred,
—Dispatched a message to the Monk, he heard
Patiently first to last, scarce shivered at,
Then curled his limbs up on his wolfskin mat
And ne'er spoke more,—informed the Ferrarese
He but retained their rule so long as these
Lingered in pupilage,—and last, no mode

Apparent else of keeping safe the road
From Germany direct to Lombardy
For Friedrich,—none, that is, to guarantee
The faith and promptitude of who should next
Obtain Sofia's dowry,—sore perplexed—
(Sofia being youngest of the tribe
[Sidenote: The next aspirant can press forward;]
Of daughters, Ecelin was wont to bribe
The envious magnates with—nor, since he sent
Henry of Egna this fair child, had Trent
Once failed the Kaiser's purposes—"we lost
Egna last year, and who takes Egna's post—
Opens the Lombard gate if Friedrich knock?")
Himself espoused the Lady of the Rock
In pure necessity, and, so destroyed
His slender last of chances, quite made void
Old prophecy, and spite of all the schemes
Overt and covert, youth's deeds, age's dreams,
Was sucked into Romano. And so hushed
He up this evening's work, that, when 't was brushed
Somehow against by a blind chronicle
Which, chronicling whatever woe befell
Ferrara, noted this the obscure woe
Of "Salinguerra's sole son Giacomo
Deceased, fatuous and doting, ere his sire,"
The townsfolk rubbed their eyes, could but admire
Which of Sofia's five was meant.

The chaps
Of earth's dead hope were tardy to collapse,
Obliterated not the beautiful
Distinctive features at a crash: but dull
And duller these, next year, as Guelfs withdrew
Each to his stronghold. Then (securely too
Ecelin at Campese slept; close by,
Who likes may see him in Solagna lie,
With cushioned head and gloved hand to denote
The cavalier he was)—then his heart smote
Young Ecelin at last; long since adult.
And, save Vicenza's business, what result
In blood and blaze? (So hard to intercept
Sordello till his plain withdrawal!) Stepped
[Sidenote: Salinguerra's part lapsing to Ecelin,]
Then its new lord on Lombardy. I' the nick
Of time when Ecelin and Alberic
Closed with Taurello, come precisely news
That in Verona half the souls refuse
Allegiance to the Marquis and the Count—
Have cast them from a throne they bid him mount,
Their Podestà, through his ancestral worth.
Ecelin flew there, and the town henceforth

Was wholly his—Taurello sinking back
From temporary station to a track
That suited. News received of this acquist,
Friedrich did come to Lombardy: who missed
Taurello then? Another year: they took
Vicenza, left the Marquis scarce a nook
For refuge, and, when hundreds two or three
Of Guelfs conspired to call themselves "The Free,"
Opposing Alberic,—vile Bassanese,—
(Without Sordello!)—Ecelin at ease
Slaughtered them so observably, that oft
A little Salinguerra looked with soft
Blue eyes up, asked his sire the proper age
To get appointed his proud uncle's page.
More years passed, and that sire had dwindled down
To a mere showy turbulent soldier, grown
Better through age, his parts still in repute,
Subtle—how else?—but hardly so astute
As his contemporaneous friends professed;
Undoubtedly a brawler: for the rest,
Known by each neighbor, and allowed for, let
Keep his incorrigible ways, nor fret
Men who would miss their boyhood's bugbear: "trap
The ostrich, suffer our bald osprey flap
A battered pinion!"—was the word. In fine,
One flap too much and Venice's marine
Was meddled with; no overlooking that!
She captured him in his Ferrara, fat
And florid at a banquet, more by fraud
Than force, to speak the truth; there 's slander laud
Ascribed you for assisting eighty years
To pull his death on such a man; fate shears
The life-cord prompt enough whose last fine thread
You fritter: so, presiding his board-head,
The old smile, your assurance all went well
With Friedrich (as if he were like to tell!)
In rushed (a plan contrived before) our friends,
Made some pretence at fighting, some amends
For the shame done his eighty years—(apart
The principle, none found it in his heart
To be much angry with Taurello)—gained
Their galleys with the prize, and what remained
But carry him to Venice for a show?
—Set him, as 't were, down gently—free to go
His gait, inspect our square, pretend observe
The swallows soaring their eternal curve
'Twixt Theodore and Mark, if citizens
Gathered importunately, fives and tens,
To point their children the Magnifico,
[Sidenote: Who, with his brother, played it out,]
All but a monarch once in firm-land, go

His gait among them now—"it took, indeed,
Fully this Ecelin to supersede
That man," remarked the seniors. Singular!
Sordello's inability to bar
Rivals the stage, that evening, mainly brought
About by his strange disbelief that aught
Was ever to be done,—this thrust the Twain
Under Taurello's tutelage,—whom, brain
And heart and hand, he forthwith in one rod
Indissolubly bound to baffle God
Who loves the world—and thus allowed the thin
Gray wizened dwarfish devil Ecelin,
And massy-muscled big-boned Alberic
(Mere man, alas!) to put his problem quick
To demonstration—prove wherever 's will
To do, there 's plenty to be done, or ill
Or good. Anointed, then, to rend and rip—
Kings of the gag and flesh-hook, screw and whip,
They plagued the world: a touch of Hildebrand
(So far from obsolete!) made Lombards band
Together, cross their coats as for Christ's cause,
And saving Milan win the world's applause.
Ecelin perished: and I think grass grew
Never so pleasant as in Valley Rù
[Sidenote: And went home duly to their reward.]
By San Zenon where Alberic in turn
Saw his exasperated captors burn
Seven children and their mother; then, regaled
So far, tied on to a wild horse, was trailed
To death through raunce and bramble-bush. I take
God's part and testify that 'mid the brake
Wild o'er his castle on the pleasant knoll,
You hear its one tower left, a belfry, toll—
The earthquake spared it last year, laying flat
The modern church beneath,—no harm in that!
Chirrups the contumacious grasshopper,
Rustles the lizard and the cushats chirre
Above the ravage: there, at deep of day
A week since, heard I the old Canon say
He saw with his own eyes a barrow burst
And Alberic's huge skeleton unhearsed
Only five years ago. He added, "June 's
The month for carding off our first cocoons
The silkworms fabricate"—a double news,
Nor he nor I could tell the worthier. Choose!

And Naddo gone, all 's gone; not Eglamor!
Believe, I knew the face I waited for,
A guest my spirit of the golden courts!
Oh strange to see how, despite ill-reports,
Disuse, some wear of years, that face retained

Its joyous look of love! Suns waxed and waned,
And still my spirit held an upward flight,
Spiral on spiral, gyres of life and light
More and more gorgeous—ever that face there
The last admitted! crossed, too, with some care
As perfect triumph were not sure for all,
[Sidenote: Good will—ill luck, get second prize:]
But, on a few, enduring damp must fall,
—A transient struggle, haply a painful sense
Of the inferior nature's clinging—whence
Slight starting tears easily wiped away.
Fine jealousies soon stifled in the play
Of irrepressible admiration—not
Aspiring, all considered, to their lot
Who ever, just as they prepare ascend
Spiral on spiral, wish thee well, impend
Thy frank delight at their exclusive track,
That upturned fervid face and hair put back!

Is there no more to say? He of the rhymes—
Many a tale, of this retreat betimes,
Was born: Sordello die at once for men?
The Chroniclers of Mantua tired their pen
Telling how Sordello Prince Visconti saved
Mantua, and elsewhere notably behaved—
Who thus, by fortune ordering events,
Passed with posterity, to all intents,
For just the god he never could become.
As Knight, Bard, Gallant, men were never dumb
In praise of him: while what he should have been,
Could be, and was not—the one step too mean
For him to take,—we suffer at this day
Because of: Ecelin had pushed away
Its chance ere Dante could arrive and take
[Sidenote: What least one may I award Sordello?]
That step Sordello spurned, for the world's sake:
He did much—but Sordello's chance was gone.
Thus, had Sordello dared that step alone,
Apollo had been compassed—'t was a fit
He wished should go to him, not he to it
—As one content to merely be supposed
Singing or fighting elsewhere, while he dozed
Really at home—one who was chiefly glad
To have achieved the few real deeds he had,
Because that way assured they were not worth
Doing, so spared from doing them henceforth—
A tree that covets fruitage and yet tastes
Never itself, itself. Had he embraced
Their cause then, men had plucked Hesperian fruit
And, praising that, just thrown him in to boot
All he was anxious to appear, but scarce

Solicitous to be. A sorry farce
Such life is, after all! Cannot I say
[Sidenote: This—that must perforce content him,]
He lived for some one better thing? this way.—
Lo, on a heathy brown and nameless hill
By sparkling Asolo, in mist and chill,
Morning just up, higher and higher runs
A child barefoot and rosy. See! the sun 's
On the square castle's inner-court's low wall
Like the chine of some extinct animal
Half turned to earth and flowers; and through the haze
(Save where some slender patches of gray maize
Are to be overleaped) that boy has crossed
The whole hill-side of dew and powder-frost
Matting the balm and mountain camomile.
Up and up goes he, singing all the while
Some unintelligible words to beat
The lark, God's poet, swooning at his feet,
So worsted is he at "the few fine locks
Stained like pale honey oozed from topmost rocks
Sun-blanched the livelong summer,"—all that 's left
Of the Goito lay! And thus bereft,
Sleep and forget, Sordello! In effect
He sleeps, the feverish poet—I suspect
[Sidenote: As no prize at all, has contented me.]
Not utterly companionless; but, friends,
Wake up! The ghost 's gone, and the story ends
I 'd fain hope, sweetly; seeing, peri or ghoul,
That spirits are conjectured fair or foul,
Evil or good, judicious authors think,
According as they vanish in a stink
Or in a perfume. Friends, be frank! ye snuff
Civet, I warrant. Really? Like enough!
Merely the savor's rareness; any nose
May ravage with impunity a rose:
Rifle a musk-pod and 't will ache like yours!
I 'd tell you that same pungency ensures
An after-gust, but that were overbold.
Who would has heard Sordello's story told.

Robert Browning – A Short Biography

He is the equal of any Victorian Poet that could be mentioned. However, Browning continues to be in the shadow of Tennyson, Arnold, Hopkins, Morris and many others.

Robert Browning was born on May 7th, 1812 in Walworth in the parish of Camberwell, London. He was baptized on June 14th, 1812, at Lock's Fields Independent Chapel, York Street, Walworth.

Browning's early years were certainly very interesting. His mother was an excellent pianist and a very devout evangelical Christian. His father, who worked as a clerk at the Bank of England, was also an artist, scholar, antiquarian, and collector of books and pictures. Indeed, he amassed more than 6,000 volumes of rare books including works in Greek, Hebrew, Latin, French, Italian, and Spanish. For the young and curious Browning, it was a wonderful resource, added to which his father was a guiding force in his education.

Many accounts attest that Browning was already proficient at reading and writing by the age of five. He is said to have been a bright but anxious student and to have studied and learnt Latin, Greek, and French by the time he was fourteen. From fourteen to sixteen he was educated at home, tutored in music, drawing, dancing, and horsemanship. Certainly, language and the arts were two areas the young Browning both absorbed and pushed himself towards.

At the age of twelve he wrote a volume of Byronic verse he called Incondita, which his parents attempted to have published. The attempts were unsuccessful and, disappointed, Browning destroyed the work.

In 1825, a cousin gave Browning a collection of Percy Bysshe Shelley's poetry; Browning was so enamored with the poems that he asked for the rest of Shelley's works for his thirteenth birthday. In fact, Browning then went the extra mile, declaring himself to be both a vegetarian and an atheist in honour of his hero.

Intriguingly it seems that the rejection of his first volume didn't dim his appreciation of other poets, but it appears to have stopped him writing any poems between the ages of thirteen and twenty.

In 1828, Browning enrolled at the newly-opened University of London. He was uncomfortable with the experience and he soon left, anxious to read and absorb at his own pace.

His education which, overall is notably rambling and lacks a structure that many of his artistic contemporaries enjoyed, i.e. excellent public schooling and then a degree at Oxford or Cambridge, may present many of his critics with ammunition to criticize, but alternatively his hap-hazard education certainly contributed to many of the references that baffled both critics and his audience, but they tellingly show the breath and scale of what he could turn words too. What others would call obscure references were, to Browning, remarkably obvious.

Browning's early career was very promising. His long poem Pauline (of which only a fragment was ever finished and published) brought him to the attention of the Pre-Raphaelite master Dante Gabriel Rossetti and his difficult Paracelsus (published in 1835) was warmly admired by both Dickens and Wordsworth.

In the 1830s he met the actor William Macready and was encouraged to develop and turn his talents to the stage by writing verse drama. But these plays, including Strafford, which ran for five nights in 1837, and those contained within the Bells and Pomegranates series, were, for the most part, unsuccessful.

During this period Browning began to discover that his real talents lay in taking a single character and allowing that character to discover more about himself by revealing further personal aspects of himself in his speeches; the dramatic monologue. The techniques he developed through this—especially the use of diction, rhythm, and symbol—are regarded as his most important contribution to poetry. They would later influence such major poets of the 20th Century as Ezra Pound, T. S. Eliot, and Robert Frost.

By 1840, with the publication of Sordello, the tide turned somewhat. Many thought he was being deliberately obscure, opaque beyond measure and his poetry for the next decade or so was not eagerly acquired or talked about.

As Browning attempted to rehabilitate his career he began a relationship with Elizabeth Barrett in 1845. He had read her poems and, being totally charmed by their quality, was determined to meet her. The poetess was better known than the younger Browning but suffered from a debilitating illness and was also subject to the harsh behaviour of her over-bearing father. Nevertheless, the new couple were soon inseparable.

Her father, as he did with any of his children that married, disinherited her. Despite this she had some money from her own resources and sensing that the best outcome for both the relationship and her own health was to move abroad the couple did just that. After a private marriage at St Marylebone Parish Church, in September 1846, they journeyed to Europe to honeymoon in Paris.

Their new life now took them to Italy, first to Pisa and a little later to Florence. There they absorbed life and one another.

But in the short term the literary assault on Browning's work did not let up. He was now criticized by such patrician writers as Charles Kingsley for his abandonment of England for foreign lands. Browning could do little to answer these attacks except to compose with his pen and continue with his poetical journey.

The Browning's were well respected, and even famous. Elizabeth health began to improve, she grew stronger and in 1849, at the age of 43, between four miscarriages, she gave birth to a son, Robert Wiedeman Barrett Browning, whom they nicknamed "Penini" or "Pen",

Intriguingly despite his growing reputation and return to form as a poet he was more often than not known as 'Elizabeth Barrett's husband'.

Work flowed from his pen that was to ensure his reputation as one of England's leading poets. When his collection Men and Women was published in 1855 it contained some of his finest lines. It was dedicated to Elizabeth. Life had begun to smile handsome rewards upon the Brownings.

Victorian society was very much taken with all things spiritualist. It was not enough to have command of much of the globe through Empire, they wished to know and explore wherever they could. The spirit world beckoned their interest. Browning dissented from this view believing it was all a hoax and a fraud. Elizabeth, however, was inclined to believe and this caused several disagreements between the couple.

They attended a séance by Daniel Dunglas Home, in July 1855. (Home was a famous and clamored after Scottish physical medium with the reported ability to levitate and speak with the dead). It is said that during this séance a spirit face materialised. Home then claimed it was the face of Browning's son who had died in infancy. Browning seized the 'materialisation' which turned out to be Home's bare foot. Browning had never lost a son in infancy.

After the séance, Browning wrote an angry letter to The Times, in which he said: "the whole display of hands, spirit utterances etc., was a cheat and imposture."

The Browning's time in Italy were immensely rewarding years for both their personal and professional lives. Browning encouraged her to include Sonnets from the Portuguese in her published works, these beautiful poems are undoubtedly one of the highlights of English love poetry.

Elizabeth had become quite politicised during these years. Engrossed in Italian politics (which was continuing to slowly re-unify the country), she issued a small volume of political poems entitled Poems before Congress (1860) most of which were written to express her sympathy with the Italian cause after the earlier outbreak of The Second Italian Independence War in 1859. In England they caused uproar. Conservative magazines such as Blackwood's and the Saturday Review labelled her a fanatic. She dedicated the book to her husband.

But in 1861 tragedy struck.

The couple had spent the winter of 1860–61 in Rome when Elizabeth's health deteriorated again and they returned to Florence in early June. However, these turned out to be her final weeks. Only morphine would now still the pain. She died in Browning's arms on June 29th, 1861. Browning said that she died "smilingly, happily, and with a face like a girl's .... Her last word was .... "Beautiful".

Her burial took place in the nearby Protestant English Cemetery of Florence. The local people were deeply saddened, and shops closed their doors in grief and respect.

Browning and their son were obviously devastated. Unable to bear being in Florence without Elizabeth they soon returned to London to live at 19 Warwick Crescent, Maida Vale.

As he re-integrated himself back into the London literary scene he began to finally receive the proper praise, respect and reputation that his works deserved.

Browning went on to publish Dramatis Personæ (1864), and The Ring and the Book (1868–1869). The latter, based on an "old yellow book" which told of a seventeenth-century Italian murder trial, received wide and generous critical acclaim. Although by now he was in the twilight of a long and prolific career, that had achieved some notable ups and downs, he was respected and indeed renowned for his talents and works.

In 1878, he revisited Italy for the first time since Elizabeth's death. He would return there on several further occasions but never to Florence.

Such was the esteem he was held in that The Browning Society was founded in 1881. Although he had never obtained a degree (something that set him apart from many other Victorian poets) he was now awarded honorary degrees from Oxford University in 1882 and then the University of Edinburgh in 1884.

In 1887, Browning produced the major work of his later years, Parleyings with Certain People of Importance in Their Day. Browning now spoke with his own voice as he engaged in a series of dialogues with long-forgotten figures of literary, artistic, and philosophic history. Unfortunately, both the critics and public were completely baffled by this.

On April 7th, 1889 Browning attended a dinner party at the home of his friend, the artist Rudolf Lehmann. The highlight of which was a recording made on a wax cylinder on an Edison cylinder phonograph. On the recording, which still exists, Browning recites part of How They Brought the Good News from Ghent to Aix, and can even be heard apologising when he forgets the words.

The recording was first played in 1890 on the anniversary of his death, at a gathering of his admirers, it was said to be the first time anyone's voice 'had been heard from beyond the grave'.

His last work Asolando: Fancies and Facts (1889), returned to his brief and concise lyric verse that was so popular. It was published on the day of his death on December 12th, 1889, Robert Browning was at his son's home Ca' Rezzonico in Venice.

He was buried in Poets' Corner in Westminster Abbey; his grave lies immediately adjacent to that of Alfred Tennyson.

Among the many who have publicly acknowledged their literary debt to him are Henry James, Oscar Wilde, George Bernard Shaw, G. K. Chesterton, Ezra Pound, Jorge Luis Borges, and Vladimir Nabokov.

Robert Browning - A Concise Bibliography

Here follows a list of the plays and poetry volumes published during his lifetime. Poems of particular worth are noted from within those volumes.

Pauline: A Fragment of a Confession (1833)
Paracelsus (1835)
Strafford (play) (1837)
Sordello (1840)
Bells and Pomegranates No. I: Pippa Passes (play) (1841)
        The Year's at the Spring
Bells and Pomegranates No. II: King Victor and King Charles (play) (1842)
Bells and Pomegranates No. III: Dramatic Lyrics (1842)
        Porphyria's Lover
        Soliloquy of the Spanish Cloister
        My Last Duchess
        The Pied Piper of Hamelin
        Count Gismond
        Johannes Agricola in Meditation
Bells and Pomegranates No. IV: The Return of the Druses (play) (1843)
Bells and Pomegranates No. V: A Blot in the 'Scutcheon (play) (1843)
Bells and Pomegranates No. VI: Colombe's Birthday (play) (1844)
Bells and Pomegranates No. VII: Dramatic Romances and Lyrics (1845)
        The Laboratory
        How They Brought the Good News from Ghent to Aix
        The Bishop Orders His Tomb at Saint Praxed's Church
        The Lost Leader
        Home Thoughts from Abroad
        Meeting at Night
Bells and Pomegranates No. VIII: Luria and A Soul's Tragedy (plays) (1846)
Christmas-Eve and Easter-Day (1850)
An Essay on Percy Bysshe Shelley (essay) (1852)
Two Poems (1854)
Men and Women (1855)
        Love Among the Ruins
        A Toccata of Galuppi's

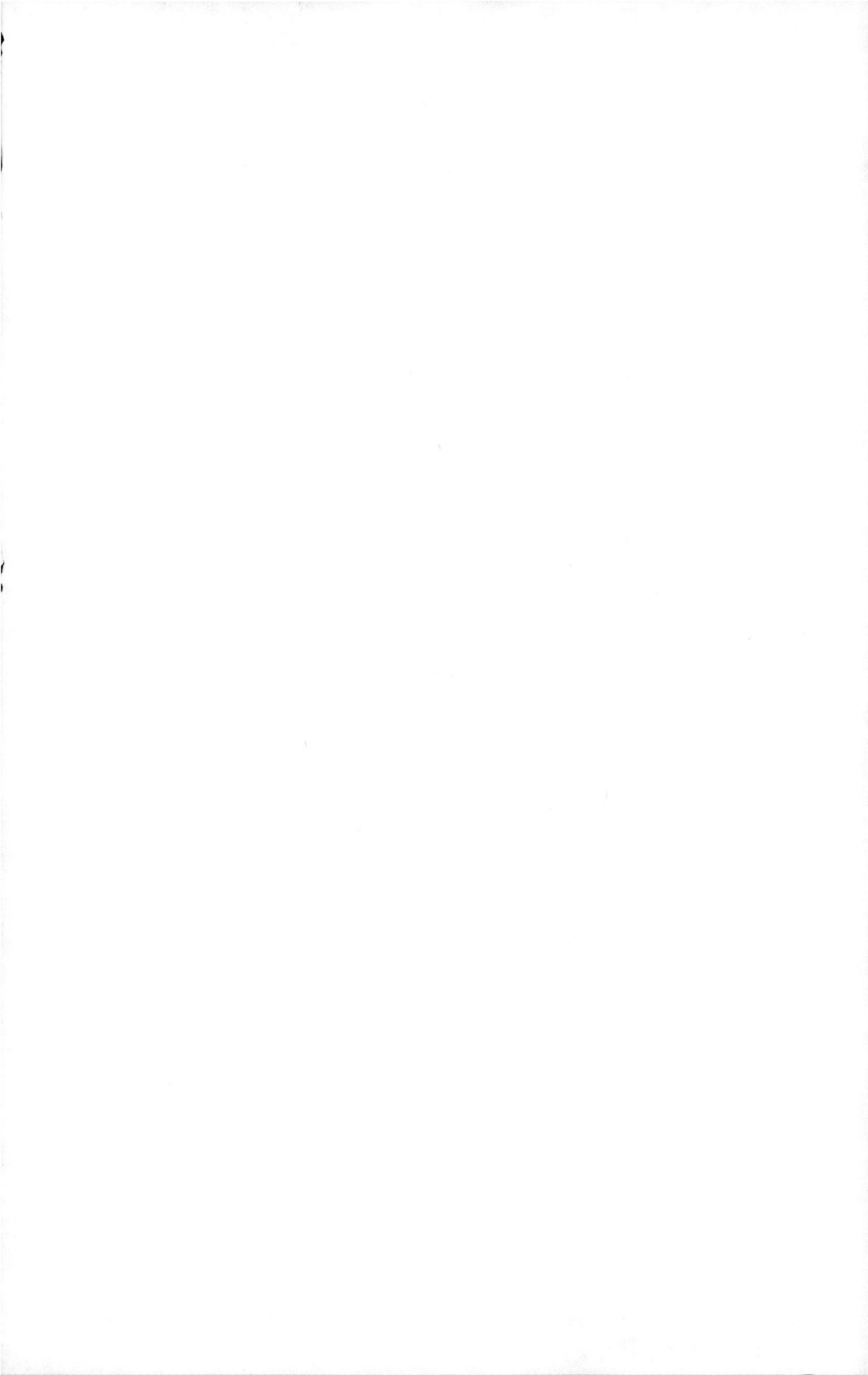

www.ingramcontent.com/pod-product-compliance
Lightning Source LLC
Chambersburg PA
CBHW060310050426
42448CB00009B/1778